Some account of the Family of Johnston or Johnson, being a pedigree, &c. of that family, drawn up by Dawson Warren, with his autograph letters on the subject to Richard Almack. 4to. 1833.

Lot 375. 20 June 1893. Sale of Sir Thomas Phillipps' Manuscripts.

THE JOURNAL OF A BRITISH
CHAPLAIN IN PARIS

The Rev.d Dawson Warren M.A.
Vicar of Edmonton in 1802.

THE JOURNAL OF A BRITISH CHAPLAIN

IN PARIS DURING THE PEACE NEGOTIATIONS OF 1801-2

From the Unpublished MS. of the Revd. Dawson Warren, M.A., unofficially attached to the Diplomatic Mission of Mr. Francis James Jackson, Edited with Notes, a Preface, and Historical Introduction by

A. M. BROADLEY

AUTHOR OF "NAPOLEON IN CARICATURE," JOINT AUTHOR OF "NAPOLEON AND THE INVASION OF ENGLAND," ETC. With Forty Illustrations, chiefly from materials collected by Mr. Dawson Warren during his sojourn in France

LONDON : CHAPMAN AND HALL, LIMITED
11 HENRIETTA STREET, COVENT GARDEN, W.C. MCMXIII

WILLIAM BRENDON AND SON, LTD., PRINTERS, PLYMOUTH

CONTENTS

APPENDICES

LIST OF ILLUSTRATIONS

FACING PAGE

EDITOR'S PREFACE

THE genesis of the hitherto unknown Dawson Warren journal which throws so much new and interesting light on the social and political condition of Paris between the arrival of the two British diplomatic missions, headed respectively by the Marquis Cornwallis and Mr. Francis James Jackson, in November, 1801, and the definite adoption of the Treaty of Amiens more than four months later, is to be found in the intimacy which commenced at St. Peter's College, Westminster, some forty years previously, between Francis Godolphin Osborne, then, and until 1789, styled Marquis of Carmarthen, and Thomas Jackson, the son of John Jackson of Chancery Lane, who was admitted to the school during the last year of the headmastership of John Nicoll in May, 1752, at the age of seven, became a King's Scholar in 1759, and was elected from Westminster to Christ Church, Oxford, in 1763. Lord Carmarthen, who was some five years Jackson's junior, came to Westminster as a " town-boy," but, by reason of the loss of the admittance book, the exact date of his arrival cannot be ascertained. His name, however, appears in the Fifth Form in the school-list for 1764, the only list of his time that has been preserved.[1] William Markham (afterwards Archbishop of York) was headmaster of Westminster from 1753 until 1764, when he was succeeded by John Hinchcliffe (subsequently Master of Trinity and Bishop of Peterborough).

Lord Carmarthen did not come to Christ Church till 11 June, 1767, and it is extremely probable that Jackson, who graduated in that year, acted for some time as his private tutor and bearleader. Two years later the young nobleman was " created " M.A., and in course of time became Chamberlain to Queen Charlotte. In after-life he did infinite credit both to Westminster and Oxford. Horace Walpole frequently alludes to his charm of form and voice, while Elizabeth Montagu describes him as " the prettiest man in his person ; the most polite and pleasing in his manners, with a sweet temper and excellent understanding happily cultivated." Between 23 Dec., 1783, and 8 June, 1791, he held the portfolio of Foreign Affairs in William Pitt's first administration, going to Paris in the spring of 1783 as Ambassador Extraordinary and Plenipotentiary. Five years later he succeeded to the dukedom. Some of his political epigrams are still remembered, amongst them the happy phrase in which, at a certain

[1] The interest of the Duke of Leeds in his old school certainly did not end with his leaving it. In 1772 he acted as Steward at the annual dinner, and on 22 April, 1790, he was elected a Busby Trustee.

crisis, he spoke of Fox as "letting the cat out of the bag to kill the rats."

It was mainly owing to the loyal friendship and good offices of Lord Carmarthen that Thomas Jackson, who had taken orders and married Charlotte Dowding, the daughter of the Vicar of Tottenham, became in rapid succession Minister of St. Botolph, Aldgate; incumbent of Seamer near Northallerton in Yorkshire and Yarlington in Somerset; Chaplain to the King and the Duke of Leeds; Prebendary of Westminster, and eventually Canon Residentiary of St. Paul's.

Charlotte Jackson kept a diary in which she murmurs plaintively at the hardness of heart which Mr. Pitt shows in not allowing her worthy husband to keep all these good things at once. When he was promoted to St. Paul's in 1792 he was obliged to resign the Westminster stall, which he had held since 1782. In 1783 he obtained the degrees of B.D. and D.D. When a son was born to Thomas and Charlotte Jackson in 1771, Lord Carmarthen and the Bishop of Worcester (Charlotte Jackson's uncle) were his god-fathers, and he was christened Francis James. Francis James Jackson was educated principally at home, but after he had entered his teens he was sent to the University of Erlangen in Bavaria, which, some twenty years later, con-ferred upon him, as British Envoy Extraordinary at Berlin, the degree of D.C.L. In 1786 Lord

Carmarthen gave his godson a clerkship in the Foreign Office, and similar good fortune befell his younger brother George, born fourteen years later, but this was not till after the death of the generous friend and patron of the family. The third child of Dr. and Mrs. Jackson was a daughter—Charlotte Lucy. Under the date 19 Jan., 1796, Mrs. Jackson writes in her journal : " My daughter Charlotte Lucy was married at Ludgate Church to the Rev. Dawson Warren, to whom Doctor J. had given the living of Edmonton.[1] Francis kissed hands on being appointed Ambassador at Constantinople." The promotion of the young diplomatist had been little less rapid than the ecclesiastical advancement of his father. Francis James Jackson was only twenty-five when he received this important appointment. His brother, born in 1785 and another plenipotentiary *in petto*, was already a Westminster scholar. Eighteen months later [30 Nov., 1797] that much-favoured churchman Canon Jackson died at Tunbridge Wells. He was only fifty-three. Mrs. Jackson writes in her diary for December : " My dear husband was interred under the great altar of St. Paul's (in the crypt) on the 10th,

---

[1] Canon Jackson entertained feelings of great regard and esteem for his son-in-law, whom he describes in the codicil of his will dated 11 Sep., 1797, as " that truly respectable character." He bequeathed to the young clergyman his gold chain and seals, as well as half his books on divinity. If George Jackson, then aged twelve, did not enter Holy Orders the Vicar of Edmonton was to have the whole of them.

MRS. DAWSON WARREN (*NÉE* CHARLOTTE LUCY JACKSON)

FROM A CONTEMPORARY WATER-COLOUR

attended by his sons and brother, and a few friends, the Duke of Leeds at the head."[1] Within two years the Duke, while still in the prime of life, was destined to follow his lifelong friend to the tomb.

It was in 1797 that the name of Bonaparte first became a terror throughout the length and breadth of the land, as the commander of the so-called Army of England. At that time it was clearly impossible to foresee the trend of events in 1801, and no one was likely to imagine that at the dawn of the new century Francis James Jackson would be named Minister Plenipotentiary to the French Republic, and that he would be accompanied to Paris by his sixteen-year-old brother, fresh from Westminster, and his brother-in-law, the versatile Vicar of Edmonton.

Between 1796 and 1798, however, Francis James Jackson had done such excellent work that Addington had no hesitation in selecting him as the head of the delicate and difficult mission to Paris, which, in the late autumn of 1801, was

[1] By his will and codicil dated respectively 16 July, 1794, and 11 Sep., 1797, Thomas Jackson bequeathed a plain mourning ring to " his ever-honoured and long-respected benefactor and friend Francis Duke of Leeds," as well as " a seal which had been given to his grace's mother by Frederick Prince of Wales," and his chrystal buttons set in gold containing the hair of the late Duchess." He left his son Francis James, the future Plenipotentiary, " his gold repeating watch, in the care of his bankers in Chancery Lane, as well as a share of all his books, pamphlets, and MSS."

b

intended to supplement the efforts of Lord Cornwallis at Amiens.[1]

If the Jacksons, father and sons, owed much
of their success in life to the friendship of

[1] It will be useful to give in a tabulated form a list of the
various posts held by Francis James Jackson during his brief
but brilliant career :—

Appointed Clerk in Foreign Office	1786
Attached to Embassy at Hague	1787
Sent home with Dutch Treaty	1788
Chargé d'Affaires to the Ministers of the States-General	
Secretary of Legation at Berlin	1789–91
Secretary of Embassy at Madrid	1792–5
Confidential Mission to Vienna	1795
Ambassador to the Ottoman Porte	1796–8
Minister Plenipotentiary to the French Republic	1801–2
Envoy Extraordinary and Minister Plenipotentiary at Berlin	1802–6
Married the daughter of the Baron du Duchat de Dorville	1803
Special Mission to Copenhagen	1808
Envoy Extraordinary and Minister Plenipotentiary to U.S.A.	1810–11

Died, 1814 ; buried, Brighton.

In the graveyard surrounding the old parish church at
Brighton there was a tomb bearing the following inscription :—

In memory of
FRANCIS JAMES JACKSON, ESQ.
Aged 43
After spending 28 of those years
honorably to himself and usefully
to his Country
His talents and firmness
as the Representative of his King
were conspicuous on
various trying occasions
His conduct in every relation of life
endeared him to all who knew him
and evinced the value of his character.

MRS. DAWSON WARREN *NÉE* CHARLOTTE
LUCY JACKSON

FROM A CONTEMPORARY SILHOUETTE IN THE POSSESSION
OF HER DESCENDANTS

THE REV. DAWSON WARREN ABOUT 1801-2

FROM A SILHOUETTE PORTRAIT IN THE POSSESSION
OF HIS DESCENDANTS

the fifth Duke of Leeds, Dawson Warren was indebted for the good living which came to him while still in deacon's orders to his fortunate father-in-law. Born on 14 Dec., 1770, Dawson Warren was the son of James Warren of Walcot House, Bath [1736–1788], and his wife Martha [1742–1798], a daughter of John Dawson.[1] James Warren was a son of John Warren of Long Melford, in Suffolk,[2] and a grandson of Rev. John Warren, Rector of Boxford [1687–1726]. Dawson Warren, in a commonplace book still possessed by his descendants, gives the following information as to the earlier portion of his career : " On the 16th Nov., 1790, I entered Trinity College, Oxford. In the course of time (1794) I took the degree of B.A., and on the 21st Dec., 1794, was ordained by the Bishop of Lincoln to the curacy of Carleton. A few months after I addressed and was accepted by my cousin Charlotte Lucy, daughter of the

[1] Martha Warren's father was a lineal descendant of the John Dawson who, in 1680, was apprenticed to George Villiers, second Duke of Buckingham, as a plate-glass blower, the secret having been brought over from Venice by the Duke. It was thus the celebrated firm of plate-glass makers Dawson, Bowles & Co. originated. A mural tablet in Edmonton Church bears the following inscription :—

MARTHA WARREN, *née* DAWSON
Entered Immortality June vi. MDCCXCVII
In her fifty-sixth year.

[2] Full particulars of the ancient family of Warren will be found in the Rev. Thomas Warren's *History and Genealogy of the Warren Family in Normandy, Great Britain and Ireland, France, Holland, Tuscany, and the United States of America,* A.D. 912–1902, privately printed twelve years ago.

Rev. Dr. Jackson, Canon Residentiary of St. Paul's. The vicarage of Edmonton became vacant on the 15th Oct., 1795, and on the 29th Nov., on the presentation of the Dean and Chapter of St. Paul's, I was admitted into priest's orders and received Institution as Vicar of Edmonton at Fulham from the Bishop of London. I took the degree of M.A. in 1797, and was appointed Chaplain to H.R.H. the Duke of York." Unlike his brother-in-law the diplomatist, Dawson Warren has found no place in the *Dictionary of National Biography*, but it was otherwise in *The Biographical Dictionary of Living Authors*.[1] The Vicar of Edmonton is mentioned not only as the translator into English verse of a Latin poem entitled *Sacerdos Parœcialis Rusticus* by the Rev. John Burton, Vicar of Mapledurham,[2] but on account of a somewhat acrimonious dispute with Mr. Robert Waithman of Farringdon Ward and Common Council of London concerning the admission of a pupil to Christ's Hospital.[3]

It is evident that the young Vicar of Edmonton was a man who was unlikely to miss the opportunity afforded him of accompanying his brother-

[1] London, 1816.
[2] *The Parish Priest: a Poem*, 4to, London. Printed by C. Whittingham and sold by A. and J. Black and other booksellers, 1800. On the title page is a vignette view of Edmonton Church, after a drawing by Dawson Warren, showing the building " before the walls were covered with brick and the Gothic stone window-frames changed for wood."
[3] A collection of pamphlets on this subject will be found in the British Museum.

MRS. DAWSON WARREN (*NÉE* CHARLOTTE LUCY JACKSON)
AND HER ELDEST DAUGHTER LOUISA

FROM A WATER-COLOUR SKETCH OF 1802

in-law to Paris at a time when the exigencies of
the first portion of the Great Terror (1796–1801)
had made it a *terra incognita* to Englishmen for
the greater part of a decade. We can well understand the desire of those whose knowledge of the
personality of " Little Boney," already the most
talked-of man in all Europe, was solely derived
from the caricatures of Gillray, Rowlandson,
Woodward and the elder Cruikshank, to see for
themselves what the First Consul was really like.
The visit to Paris marked an epoch in the life of
Dawson Warren and the history of his family.
In 1800 four children had already been born to
the Vicar of Edmonton and Mrs. Warren, who had
also inherited a large share of the personal attractions for which her brother, the Minister Plenipotentiary to France, was remarkable.   In the
contemporary portrait now reproduced she is
portrayed in the company of her eldest child
Louisa [1796–1862], who, in 1824, married the
Rev. Thomas Durham, Curate of Burton Latimer.
The other children born prior to the expedition to
Paris were Charlotte [1798–1889], Amelia [1799–
1869], and Dawson [1800–1838].   It is to his
great-grandson Colonel Dawson Warren, now in
command of the Queen's Royal West Surrey Regiment, that the journal which the Rev. Dawson
Warren eventually drew up in diary form from the
numerous letters which he addressed day by day
to his wife at Edmonton now belongs.   It is

probable that the writer all along contemplated the possibility of publishing an account of all he saw in Paris before the final conclusion of the Treaty of Amiens on 27 March, 1802, made France and her capital accessible to a wholesale invasion of English visitors, which included personages of distinction like Fox, Sheridan, Erskine, Mackintosh, the sisters Mary and Agnes Berry, Mrs. Damer, and the Cosways, as well as clerks and shopkeepers.

The Rev. Dawson Warren left England for Paris on 12 Nov., 1801, and returned to Edmonton on 29 Jan., 1802. Mr. Jackson did not reach England until 24 April, 1802. From 1802 until his death, nearly thirty-seven years later, the Vicar of Edmonton seems to have led an uneventful life amongst admiring parishioners, some of whom may possibly have seen John Gilpin in the days when the village still retained its pristine rusticity untarnished. In 1813, on the death of the Rev. Thomas Wimbolt, the Rev. Dawson Warren took possession of Sir John Weld's Chapel at Southgate as appurtenant to the vicarage of Edmonton. Between 1802 and 1816 nine other children were born at the old vicarage, which, like its neighbour the original Bell Inn, made world-famous by Cowper, has now been demolished.[1]

[1] 5. Anne [1802–1878] m. Major Thomas John Hammond [1791–1875], and the mother of the Rev. Canon Hammond, Col. Sir Arthur G. Hammond, v.c., k.c.b., and Dr. William

THE WRITER OF THE PARIS JOURNAL AND HIS FAMILY IN THE PARLOUR OF EDMONTON VICARAGE.

FROM A SKETCH MADE BY MARIA GIBERNE ABOUT 1830.

Towards the end of his life, while arranging his journal, with scrupulous care as to detail, and placing in it the various items of interest he had collected for its illustration long years before in Paris, the diarist seems to have entertained some misgivings as to whether the curiosity which prompted his joining the Jackson mission was justifiable.

The Editor is anxious to express his thanks to Miss Gertrude Rosalie Henderson of St. Leonards, the granddaughter of the eldest child of the Rev. Dawson Warren, who has ar-

Hammond, Librarian of the Grand Lodge of Freemasons, and other children. Major Hammond's brother Dr. Hammond, who died a nonagenarian in 1907, after his evidence had been taken by commission in the Druce case, was the eighth medical man of the same family practising in succession at Edmonton. John Keats was apprenticed to one of the Hammonds. 6. Rev. Edward Blackburn [1803–1894], sometime Vicar of St. Mary's, Marlborough. 7. Frederick [b. and d. 1805]. 8. Lucy [1806–1823]. 9. Rev. Charles [1808–1883]. 10. Francis [1810–1880]. 11. Selina [1812–1879]. 12. Susanna [1814–1896], and Frederick Skinner [1816–1887]. His widow Georgina, daughter of Leon Simpson, is still alive. In Edmonton Church a mural tablet, ornamented with the Warren arms and the device *Curre ut vincas*, bears the following inscription :—

In the memory of
DAWSON WARREN, M.A.
Forty-three years Vicar of this parish
who after faithfully preaching the gospel
and adorning it by a devout and holy life
by a paternal attention to the wants of his flock
especially in the charitable instruction of the young
and by kindness, meekness and courtesy towards all
entered into his rest on the 17th day of Decr. A.D. 1838,
in the sixty-ninth year of his age.
This monument was erected by his grateful parishioners,
as a token of affectionate regard.

ranged in a large album a series of portraits, together with an important collection of MSS. relating to the Warren, Dawson, and Jackson families and their kinsfolk. Mrs. Henderson, the daughter of Louisa Durham, *née* Warren (born in 1796), and the granddaughter and namesake of Charlotte Lucy Warren, *née* Jackson (the bride of 1795), is still living and takes the keenest interest in all matters relating to the family history. When a child she often stayed at Edmonton Vicarage, and still entertains a pleasant recollection of her genial grandfather, who addressed to her the playful letter now in her daughter's collection.

The Editor has also received valuable assistance from Dr. William Hammond, Librarian of the Grand Lodge of Freemasons ; the Rev. G. H. Nall, Librarian of Westminster School, and Mr. G. F. Russell Barker, the standard authority on all matters relating to that ancient foundation. To M. Auguste Geoffroy, of 5 Rue Blanche, Paris, whose expert knowledge of eighteenth-century prints is probably unrivalled, he owes several valuable illustrations and much useful information, as well as the loan of the medal so effectively reproduced by Messrs. Chapman & Hall on the covers of this volume. Useful information has also been given him by M. Hector Fleischmann and Mr. G. L. de St. M. Watson.

The text of the Rev. Dawson Warren has been

THE REV. DAWSON WARREN AND HIS FAMILY IN THE ARBOUR OF EDMONTON
VICARAGE GARDEN.

FROM A SKETCH MADE BY MARIA GIBERNE 1830.

followed as closely as possible, although it has been necessary to suppress a large number of the capital letters which, after the fashion of the age in which he lived, he uses on every possible occasion.

Explanatory notes have been added whenever necessary for the elucidation of the narrative.

It has been deemed advisable to add by way of an Appendix a small section of the lively diary of George Jackson, the brother of the Minister Plenipotentiary, and his unpaid attaché,[1] which brings the story which his brother-in-law Mr. Dawson Warren commences down to the actual signing of the Treaty of Amiens and the termination of the Jackson mission. To this have also been added a few notes of identification. The other appendices consist of the text of the Peace Preliminaries of 1 Oct., 1801, and Bonaparte's Peace Proclamation of 1 Nov. of the same year, and a short pedigree of the descendants of the Rev. Dawson Warren, which has been supplied by Miss Gertrude R. Henderson.

A. M. BROADLEY.

19 *July*, 1913.

[1] See *post*, p. 221.

HISTORICAL INTRODUCTION

THE first two years of the nineteenth century have been described from a French point of view as an *entr'acte* between the bloodshed of the Revolution and the battles of the Empire. In the annals of the British Empire they form a prelude to the twelve years' struggle which began at the end of 1803 and ended only with Waterloo, the centenary of which is now within measurable distance. The journal of the Rev. Dawson Warren affords a new and vivid picture of both French and English political and social life in Paris between the middle of November, 1801, and the end of January, 1802. Before the year 1801 was three months old Pitt had retired from the office[1] he had held ever since 1783, and Henry Addington, called by James Gillray, " Peter Pindar," and his detractors " the Doctor," reigned in his stead. In the Addington Cabinet the all-important position of Minister of Foreign Affairs fell to Robert Banks Jenkinson [1770–1829], the son and successor of Charles Jenkinson [1727–1808], who between 1796 and his father's death bore the courtesy title of Lord Hawkesbury. From 14 February, 1799, until the

[1] 14 March, 1801.

spring of 1801 he had held, under Pitt, the office of Master of the Mint.

When Addington took office in March, 1801, the French Consulate, of which Napoleon Bonaparte was something more than the figure-head, had been in existence just sixteen months. From " the day of Brumaire " (9 Nov., 1799) onwards the little Corsican we feared and lampooned, had marched from victory to victory, but England still remained unconquered and unconquerable. She had spent money lavishly in promoting the coalitions of 1793 and 1799, and had made heroic preparations for the defence of the country on land, as well as by sea, if the long-threatened invasion of her shores ever took place. George III was prepared to lead his troops in person against the man we called derisively " Little Boney," and a similar spirit animated all classes of the community. The national feeling of 1799–1801 is still reflected in countless songs, broadsides, leaflets, and caricatures.[1] It is certain that Bonaparte was far more anxious to bring about a peace with England in the early part of 1801 than he had been in the previous year, during which he had triumphed over the Austrians and the Second Coalition at Marengo (14 June). Nearly the whole

[1] For a full account of the condition of affairs in England prior to the signing of the Peace Preliminaries on 1 Oct., 1801, see *Napoleon and the Invasion of England : The Story of the Great Terror.* Vol. I, pp. 1–194. By H. F. B. Wheeler and A. M. Broadley. John Lane. 1908.

of the possessions of France *in partibus* were in the hands of England, and their surrrender was essential before Bonaparte could give any practical shape to the schemes for the restoration of the French Colonial Empire which now occupied his attention. The news he had received from Egypt was of so disquieting a nature as to make the peace question one of considerable urgency. Very little is known of the negotiations which lasted throughout the spring and summer of 1801 between Lord Hawkesbury and Monsieur Louis William Otto [1754–1817], whose ostensible occupation in London was the arranging of terms for the exchange of prisoners of war. Otto was a native of Baden, who, in early life, had been employed by M. de la Luzerne " in the diplomatic line " in America as well as in England. His first wife was an American lady, Miss Livingston, possibly a relation of the Councillor Robert Livingston, the American envoy to France, who arrived at Paris at the end of 1801.[1] In 1782 he had married, as his second wife, the daughter of the French Consul at New York. Otto was a man of good presence and manners. That he was in affluent circumstances is made clear by the fact that during the year 1801 he occupied the handsome corner house at the eastern end of Hereford Street, on the southern side of Oxford Street and close to Portman Square, then generally called

[1] See *post*, p. 4.

EXCHANGE OF THE RATIFICATION OF THE PRELIMINARIES OF PEACE
AGREED TO ON OCTOBER 1, 1801, BETWEEN M. OTTO AND LORD HAWKESBURY

FROM A CONTEMPORARY ENGRAVING

Oxford Road. Little or nothing was allowed to leak out concerning the progress of the negotiations either by Mr. Addington and Lord Hawkesbury on the one hand or Monsieur Otto on the other. England and France were still technically in a state of war on Thursday, 1 October, 1801, when late in the afternoon the preliminaries of peace which were to form the basis of the Treaty of Amiens were signed by Lord Hawkesbury on behalf of George III and Monsieur Otto as the representative of the French Republic. *The London Gazette* of Friday, 2 October, contains the following official announcement :—

"DOWNING-STREET, OCT. 2.

" PRELIMINARIES of Peace between his Majesty and the French Republic were signed last night at Lord Hawkesbury's Office, in Downing-street, by the Right Honourable Lord Hawkesbury, one of his Majesty's Principal Secretaries of State, on the part of his Majesty, and by M. Otto, on the part of the French Government."

On the previous evening Addington had found time to communicate the intelligence to William Windham,[1] who at once replied :—

" I must not omit to thank you for your note, however dreadful the intelligence it contains . . . *the Country has received its death blow.*"

In his valuable work, *Itinéraire Général de*

[1] See *Windham Papers*, 1903. Vol. II, p. 172.

Napoléon Ier, under the date of 1 October, 1801, M. Albert Schuermans gives us the following information :—

" À la Malmaison. Le Premier Consul reçoit la nouvelle de la signature de la paix d'Amiens entre la France et l'Angleterre."

It is almost incredible that this intelligence could have reached Paris before the following day, and the agreement arrived at in Downing Street can hardly be described as the Treaty of Amiens. Possibly the news may have been transmitted by the semaphore-telegraph, but in any case Bonaparte did not conceal his satisfaction at the diplomatic success scored by Otto. Councils were held every day, and on Sunday, 4 October, the following notification was officially published :—

" Extract from the Registers of the Deliberations of the Consuls of the Republic, Paris, Oct. 4.
    " THE consuls of the republic having heard the council of state, decree—
    " 1st. That on the 9th of November next, there shall be celebrated, throughout the whole of the republic, a solemn festival on account of the signing of peace between England and France.
    " 2. The minister of the interior is charged with the execution of this decree.
                        " (Signed) BONAPARTE,
                            H. B. MARET, sec. state."

Nothing could well be better timed or more dramatic. The 9 November of the Gregorian

than on questions of detail concerning mutual concessions, in which respect France undeniably came off best both on 1 October, 1801, and 27 March, 1802.

In view of what happened within twenty short months it is curious to read such an account of the jubilation of 10 October, 1801, as the following :—

" In London, the ratification, has produced the most general and voluntary demonstrations that could be expressed of heart-felt satisfaction for peace, so unexpectedly and honourably obtained. The streets were one continued blaze of light, and many beautiful and significant transparent subjects were displayed. The following are among those which deserve particular notice : the Navy-office, Somerset-house—G. R. and the anchor, &c. in variegated lamps. The Theatres with brilliant variegated lamps ; inscriptions Peace, and emblems of the Cornucopia, which, indeed, was the prevailing design. India house—G. R. with Peace in capitals, and a great number of lamps. Mansion house—the Crown and G. R. Guildhall—the Crown and G. R. with a small transparency, the dove encompassed with olive. Excise-office—G. R. and Crown, with a number of lamps. Phœnix Fire-office—a transparency, Long live the King, Peace and Commerce. Post-office—a great number of lamps. Bank—a few lamps in some of the windows. The Lyceum—a transparency, Peace and Plenty surmounting War and Monopoly. Sir Vere Hunt's, corner of Parliament-street, facing

Whitehall—France and Ireland, with England entwining the horn of plenty. The dukes of York and Portland had a number of flambeaus on the outer parapet walls. Oakley's furniture warehouse, in Bond-street—displayed a good design, well executed, of Peace, Plenty, and Commerce. Orme's gallery—Britannia crowning a sailor and Soldier Youth with Laurel.

" During the rejoicings the most tremendous storm of thunder, lightning, and rain came on, which soon dispersed the crowds that were abroad. —The lightning preceded the thunder and rain full one hour, and was uncommonly vivid. The day had been unusually fine, and warm for the season of the year. The storm lasted till toward three o'clock yesterday morning."

Very few of the London illuminators seem to have surpassed M. Otto either in elaboration of design or lavishness of expenditure, and the appearance of his house in Hereford Street attracted enormous crowds. " It presented," says the reporter of the *Morning Chronicle*, " three sides to the view. On the north was displayed a large letter P in a circular wreath ; on the west was a large transparency with the words ' Peace and Universal Happiness,' with a civic crown in the midst. Under this and extending along the entire front was a double festoon of lights, from the bow at the top of which rose the stem of an olive tree, which, twisting in various shapes, shot out at its extremity a single green branch ; the

NAPOLEON, FIRST CONSUL
FROM A PRINT OF 1802

drops of the festoon terminated at the north side of the hall door in the letters G. R., and on the south side in F. R. The south side was emblazoned with a star composed of red, white, and blue lights, besides several smaller compartments of lights." M. Otto was certainly the man of the hour, and M. Lauriston shared his popularity.

A glazier in Shoreditch wishing to compliment the representative of the Consulate put in his transparency the lines :—

> " Let's drink their health, by way of motto.
> Here's to Lord Hawkesbury and Monsieur Otto."

On the afternoon of the eventful 10 October, Cobbett again wrote from Pall Mall to Mr. Windham at Norwich :—

" The guns are now firing for the Peace. Half an hour ago a very numerous crowd drew the *Aide-de-Camp of Bonaparte in triumph through Pall Mall!* The vile miscreants had, it seems, watched his motions very narrowly, and perceiving him get into a carriage in Bond Street with Otto, they took out the horses, dragged him down that street, down St. James's Street, along by your house, down to White-hall, and through the Park, and then to Otto's again, shouting and rejoicing every time he had occasion to get out of his carriage. The modest sansculotte bore all this with great complacency."[1]

The sturdy proprietor of *The Porcupine* was

---

[1] Melville's *Cobbett.* Vol. I, p. 131.

compelled to illuminate by the mob *malgré lui*, and the example he endeavoured to set was certainly not imitated in the provinces, which shared to a very great extent the enthusiasm of London. In 1801 Greville and Creevey had not commenced their note-taking, and the other chroniclers of small talk are provokingly silent on the subject of the Peace. Miss Berry was so busy over the production of " Fashionable Friends " at Strawberry Hill that she does nothing more than record the fact that on 14 October Joanna Baillie, while sending " a plain, simple prologue of no pretentions," wrote from Hampstead :—

" I hope you receive pleasure from this blessed prospect of peace. I have rejoiced heartily, and paid for our clay and candles with no begrudging spirit."[1]

It was not until November that the mistress of Holland House found time to write :—

" Peace has been made. Pitt continues supporting Ministers ; the Grenvilles are in open opposition. Grey gave up Fox with a quibble ; the others excluded Sheridan. Fox was given up shamefully."

On Saturday, 3 October, Madame d'Arblay wrote to her father at Chelsea, " God avert

[1] *Extracts of the Journals and Correspondence of Miss Berry* [1783–1852], edited by Lady Theresa Lewis. Vol. II, p. 116.

mischief from this Peace,"[1] but she gives us a very amusing account of her husband's interview with his old friend and fellow-soldier General Lauriston in the neighbourhood of St. James's Street. As a result of the interview General Comte d'Arblay started for France on 6 November, and his wife followed him five months later.

On the very day of the ratification the following decree was signed in Paris :—

" Decree of Oct. 10.
" Bonaparte, first consul of the republic, decrees :—
" Article 1. Citizen Joseph Bonaparte, counsellor of state, be appointed minister plenipotentiary of the republic at the congress of Amiens.
"2. The minister for foreign affairs is charged with the execution of the present decree.
" The first consul,
" (Signed)   BONAPARTE.
" Paris, Oct. 12."

Ten days later the First Consul approved a second decree as a practical result of the first :—

" The consuls of the republic, on the report of the minister of war, decree as follows :
" 1. The artillery and fortifications of the military positions all along the frontiers of the republic shall be placed on the peace establishment.

[1] *Diary and Letters of Madame d'Arblay*, edited and annotated by Austin Dobson (1903). Vol. V, pp. 505–6.

" 2. The minister at war is charged with the execution of the present decree.

" The chief consul,

" (Signed)   BONAPARTE.

"H. B. MARET, sec. of state."

While the Parisians waited with such patience as they could command for the fireworks and festivities of 18 Brumaire, the First Consul, in the new rôle of general peacemaker, ordered quite a number of medals to be struck in honour of the new relations he had established with King George and his subjects.[1]   On more than one of these appears the somewhat equivocal device *Je retiens la foudre et accepte la paix.*   In the *Gazette de France* of 12 Vendémaire (3 Oct., 1801) one reads : " Aujourd'hui, vers 7 heures du soir, le bruit du canon s'est fait entendre a plusieurs reprises et pendant longtemps.   À neuf heures, les commissaires de police escortés de plusieurs détachements de cavalerie et infantrie ont publié dans toutes les places et carrefours de Paris, et au son d'une musique guerrière, la signatures des préliminaires de la paix avec Angleterre."   Bonaparte pinned his faith to the date he had chosen for his official pronouncement, and it was not till 9 November, when Lord Cornwallis had arrived in Paris and Mr. Francis James Jackson was making his last preparations for crossing over to France,

---

[1] See *Médailler Napoléon le Grand.* L. Bramsen, 1904. pp. 27–37.

FRANCIS JAMES JACKSON, BRITISH MINISTER PLENIPOTENTIARY
AT PARIS, NOV. 1801–APRIL 1802
FROM A MEZZOTINT OF THE PERIOD

Tuileries in the full canonicals of an Anglican divine.[1]

That considerable importance was attached by Bonaparte to the Jackson mission there can be little doubt. Amongst the relics of their ancestors treasured by the lineal descendants of the young Minister Plenipotentiary of 1801–2 and his Chaplain and brother-in-law is an official copy of a letter, engrossed on parchment " with highly embellished penmanship ", and addressed by the First Consul on 5 May, 1802, to H.M. King George III. It runs thus :—

" Au nom du Peuple Français
" Bonaparte Premier Consul
" à sa Majesté Britannique.
" J'ai reçu la lettre par laquelle Votre Majesté m'informe qu'elle a jugé àpropos de rappeler auprès d'elle le sieur François Jacques Jackson son Ministre Plenipotentière auprès de la Republique Française. La conduite sage et prudente qu'il a tenu pendant la course de la mission qu'il vient de remplir içi, lui a mérité la plus entière approbation de ma part, et c'est avec plaisir que je lui en rends ce témoignage.

" Je ne doute pas après son retour auprès de Votre Majesté il ne soit empressé de vous transmettre tout ce que je lui ai laissé connaître de mes sentimens personnels et de ma disposition bien sincère à concourir sans cesse au maintien de l'union et de la bonne intelligence, si heureuse-

[1] See *post*, p. 163.

ment rétablie entre les deux Nations, aussi de vous donner de nouvelles assurances des vœux que je forme pour la prospérité de Votre Majesté.

" Donné à Paris au Palais du Gouvernement le quinze floréal an dix de le République Française Cinq Mai mil huit cent deux.

" BONAPARTE
" le Premier Consul
" Par le secrétaire d'État
" EUGÈNE MARET

" Le Ministre de
 " Relations Extérieures
  Ch : M. de Talleyrand."

It is, however, principally from a social point of view that the journal of the Rev. Dawson Warren possesses an enduring human interest. Between 1793 and 1801 comparatively few Englishmen or Englishwomen had visited the French capital. The still beautiful Margravine of Anspach came there, under what she was pleased to call " a neutral flag," before the peace negotiations had taken a tangible shape, and Lady Holland speaks of the presence there of Lord Wycombe, the future Marquis of Lansdowne, in the early months of 1801, but these were exceptions to the rule. A certain number of English travellers crossed the Channel in the winter of 1801–2, but it was not till after the return of Lord Cornwallis to England that Paris regained the popularity it enjoyed in the pre-Revolution days with English tourists. Of the Paris of March–December, 1802, one

PARIS IN 1801–2

FROM THE CONTEMPORARY AQUATINT OF L. P. DEBUCOURT

catches many interesting glimpses in the journals
of both Madame d'Arblay and Mary Berry, but
somehow or other we know less of Paris during
the interval which elapsed between the Brumaire
which gave Bonaparte the power he longed for,
and the Brumaire at which he posed as the giver
of peace to Europe, than we know of the Paris of
the Convention and the Directory. From November, 1799, onwards nearly every class of Parisian
society showed a strong inclination to rebel against
the worst features of the Revolution, but certain
eccentricities of costume still prevailed, and these
are admirably portrayed in the colour-prints of
the aquatintist Louis Philibert Debucourt (De
Bucourt before the great social upheaval of 1789–
1793), who was born in the reign of Louis XV and
lived to see the advent to power of Louis Philippe.
From the famous series known as " Manners and
Absurdities of the Day " we are able to realize the
scenes which both Dawson Warren and George
Jackson describe so minutely in their respective
journals. Many of Debucourt's engravings and
the caricatures of Martinet, who already flourished
in the Rue du Coq, St. Honoré, are reproduced in
the chapters devoted to the first two years of the
nineteenth century in Charles Simond's wonderful
book on Paris between 1800 and 1900.[1]   In this

[1] *La Vie Parisienne à travers le xixe siècle*. Paris de 1800
à 1900 d'après les estampes et les mémoires du temps. Paris :
Libraire Plon, 1900. Vol. I, pp. 18–54.

book we have contemporary views showing the churches, the botanical gardens, the quays, the city gates and the Tuileries gardens exactly as they were when the Jacksons visited them in the company of Dawson Warren, Hill, and Webb. Even at the beginning of 1801 Bonaparte had the Empire in view, and very possibly that dream of absolute power had a great deal to do with his sudden passion for peace. He was already busy with his schemes of legislative and administrative reform, and was strengthening his relations with both the Pope and the *émigrés*. Rabid Jacobinism was rapidly losing ground, and the terms *Citoyen* and *Citoyenne*, as well as the use of the Republican Calendar, were becoming unpopular. It was an era of riotous living, unbridled pleasure, and self-indulgence, and if the dresses in which the Vicar of Edmonton saw Mesdames Tallien and Récamier were a trifle less diaphanous than those which suited the taste of Barras, Ouvrard and others, they were cut low enough to shock the worthy divine, who appeared at the Tuileries in cap, gown, hood and bands, and was the first " minister of any denomination " to perform a religious service publicly without fear of condign punishment, since both Religion and the Deity were abolished by a decree clothed in legal form.

Dawson Warren's sojourn in Paris came to an end just two months before the Marquis Cornwallis returned to London to read and hear all the

evil things which were written and said of the
treaty he had concluded with so much trouble and
vexation.[1]   At St. Helena Napoleon bestowed a
few commendatory epithets on the sexagenarian
ambassador, but he forgot to say anything about
the young Minister Plenipotentiary of whom he
had written so appreciatively to George III.   He
had survived them both.   When Napoleon died
in 1821, Francis James Jackson, " dead before his
prime," had slept for seven years in Brighton
churchyard, and India had raised a monument to
Lord Cornwallis, who only three years after he
had quitted Amiens died at Ghazipore while
attempting to render one more important service
to the country he had so long served in both
hemispheres.

[1] Napoleon at once ordered a medal to be designed by
Dumarest, bearing his own laurel-crowned head in profile and
the words Napoleon Bonaparte, First Consul.   On the reverse
is a figure of Victory offering an olive branch to recumbent
Britannia wearing a naval crown.   Above are the words " Paix
d'Amiens "—below   the   date   " vi   Germinal   An   x—xxvii
March 1802."   Little more than a year later Denon and Jeuffroy
were charged with the execution of a second medal, upon which
is portrayed a leopard of forbidding aspect in the act of destroying
a document.   Above it is the legend : " The Treaty of Amiens
broken by England in May of the Year 1803," and on the reverse
a female equestrian figure—apparently a winged Victory.   Round
this side of the medal runs the inscription : " Hanover occupied
by the French army in June 1803."   Below the horse : " Struck
with silver from the mines of Hanover. *The year* 4 *of Bonaparte.*"

LOUIS G. OTTO,
PLENIPOTENTIARY of the FRENCH REPUBLICK
in GREAT BRITAIN 1801.

PORTRAIT OF LOUIS WILLIAM OTTO

FROM THE ENGRAVING OF PHILLIPS AFTER JUKES, LONDON, OCTOBER, 1801

MY PARIS JOURNAL

MY PARIS JOURNAL

NOVEMBER, 1801–FEBRUARY, 1802

Our Departure from London

HAVING accepted the invitation of my brother-in-law [Mr. Francis James Jackson] to accompany him to Paris I waited on the Citizen Otto,[1] who resided in London as Consul of the

---

[1] A brief account of Louis William Otto will be found in the Introduction. In Nov., 1801, he enjoyed a large share of popularity, and on 1 Jan., 1802, a good engraved portrait of him (now reproduced) by S. Philipps after a picture by Jukes, for which Otto gave sittings, was published by Samuel Philipps of Savile House, Leicester Square. He must have possessed a very fair knowledge of English, as is evidenced by the following holograph letter, now in possession of the editor of this journal :—

> "HEREFORD STREET, [OXFORD ROAD],
> "*Dec.* 5, 1801.
> "SIR,
> "I have received the Box you have been so good as to send me for the first Consul and I shall with great pleasure forward it by the first opportunity.
> "Permit me to add my best thanks for the Prints you have done me the honour to address. I shall take advantage of the first leisure hour to wait upon you and see your collection.
> "Sir,
> "Your very obedient and very humble servant,
> "OTTO."

Before the end of the year M. Otto appears to have received credentials which gave him the same diplomatic rank in London which Mr. Jackson held in Paris. In 1802 he moved from Hereford Street to 29 Portman Square.

French Government, to request a passport. He returned my visit, and invited me to dinner. I there met Mr. Jackson and a party of about twenty. Among them was that extraordinary character the Chevalière D'Éon.[1] She was dressed as an elderly woman and full of life and spirits. When the ladies retired from the table, she returned, tapped at the door, and offered to sit half an hour longer with the gentlemen. She was exceedingly entertaining, and told many anecdotes with great spirit and humour. Madame Otto was an American[2] and a most beautiful woman. She sent to Josephine the wife of the First Consul a present of an English cap.

[This dinner took place on Nov. 5, for on the following day Mr. George Jackson, fresh from Westminster, wrote a lively account of it to his mother, to whom he laughingly accords permission to " talk about *our* mission at the Bath tea-tables to her heart's content." In his letter of 23 October the head of that mission had enjoined silence and discretion.[3] " I think it will please

---

[1] Charles Geneviève Louis Auguste André Thimothée d'Éon, b. 5 Oct., 1728, d. 21 May, 1810. It was proved conclusively by a post-mortem examination that the so-called Chevalière belonged to the male sex. M. Otto granted d'Éon a passport to return to France, but his affairs were too deeply involved to allow of his leaving England.

[2] M. Otto's first wife was Miss Livingston, an American lady, but the lady Mr. Dawson Warren must have seen was a daughter of M. de St. Jean Crevecour, French Consul at New York, who married Otto in 1782.

[3] See *ante*, Introduction, p. xxviii.

you, dearest M," writes the unpaid attaché of sixteen on 6 Nov.,[1] " to hear that I have eaten what I call my first diplomatic dinner. I need hardly explain that it was not at Mr. Addington's, nor at Lord Hawkesbury's. It was at M. Otto's, the French Chargé d'Affaires. My brother and Mr. Webb only were invited ; but when M. Otto, who called to speak with Francis on business, heard that I too was going to Paris, he begged that my brother would allow me also to dine with them (Mr. Dawson Warren must also have been included in the invitation). He and his wife, an American lady, are both very pleasant people, perhaps what you would call of the old school, for they are excessively polite, and unlike in manners what I should have expected to find citizens of either the modern republics. We had, however, in a very lively lady just arrived from Paris, a specimen of the new French school, both in dress and deportment. Perhaps she would have shocked you a little, but she amused us a good deal. There was also of the party a great *célébrité* Mademoiselle d'Éon, the famous chevalier, who served as a man, for nearly forty years, in the French service.[2] My brother told me he remembered paying at Bath,

---

[1] *Diaries and Letters of Sir George Jackson.* London, 1872. Vol. I, pp. 89.

[2] Some thirty-five years before, the Chevalier d'Éon had been for a short time the duly accredited representative of Louis XV at the Court of St. James's. The bills of his Bath performances are still in existence.

in 1795, a half-crown to see her take part in a
public exhibition of fencing. Our dinner was a
very handsome one ; and of course in the French
style—everything *très recherché*. The French and
English flags floated together over the central
plateau, and we drank prosperity and stability to
their union in foaming bumpers of champagne.

" I spent two days at the Hotel in Albemarle
Street.[1] On Tuesday 10 November, after the
carriages had waited some hours at the door, the
final orders came from the Foreign Office, and we
went to a late dinner at Dartford and there we
slept."]

My first letter to my loved Correspondent was
from Dartford, the second from Dover. There is
nothing in them to transcribe. I complained of a
large bandbox containing Madame Bonaparte's
cap, and a very enormous package for Lord Cornwallis which occupied too large a portion of the
second carriage in which I travelled, Mr. Jackson
and Mr. Webb occupying the first. At Dover we
met a messenger from Lord Cornwallis which
induced Mr. Jackson to stop the mail till he had
written to the Foreign Office. From this messenger I learnt that his Lordship had been
well received by the inhabitants of France who
saluted him with cannon, and illuminations, and
shouted " Vivent les Anglais."

---

[1] The York Hotel and Coffee House, which then belonged to
M. Dorant, the proprietor of another hotel in Jermyn Street.

No. 41.

Par autorifation fpeciale du Premier Conful de la Republique Francoife.

⁘⸭⸭═⸭⸭⸭

Le Commissaire du Gouvernement Francois en Angleterre,

PRIE tous ceux qui font à prier de laiſſer paſſer librement et en toute fureté

le rév.ᵈ Moᵘʳˢ Warren

Natif de *Londres* agé de *trente un* Cheveux et

fourcils *noirs* Yeux *noirs* Front *bas*

nez *petit* Menton *court* Viſage *honnête* Allant

en France

fans donner ni fouffrir qu'il foit donné aucun empéchement.

Le prefent Paſſeport valable pour *trois* _____ Decades feulement.

Donné à Londres le *dix neuf Brumaire* an *dix* de la Republique Francoife une et indiviſible.

Signature du porteur

Dawson Warren

Par le Commiſſaire.

Arthur Abeline

Gratis.

FACSIMILE OF PASSPORT GRANTED TO REV. DAWSON WARREN
BY M. OTTO, FRENCH PLENIPOTENTIARY IN LONDON,
DATED NOV. 10, 1807

[Mr. George Jackson gives a somewhat different version of the manner in which the British Minister Plenipotentiary was entrusted with the conveyance of the headdress for the wife of the First Consul. He writes :—

" We left London yesterday at 8 a.m. At Dartford we were overtaken by a messenger sent in pursuit of us by Madame Otto, from whom he brought a note, and a small box that had been taken to our hotel almost immediately after we left it. The box was recommended to my brother's especial care, its important contents being a cap for Madame Bonaparte. After promising that the millinery should be well looked after, we posted on with all speed and arrived here (Dover) to dinner."]

From Dover to Paris

The following is the first letter I wrote from Paris, 18 Nov., 1801.[1]

My dear Charlotte,

My last from Dover was closed most abruptly by a notice sent from the Post Office that the mail would not wait a moment longer. The departure of the mail finished the business of my companions, and allowed us to enjoy our dinner. The next morning I walked round Dover while the

[1] It must be remembered that it was not until 1834 that Mr. Dawson Warren arranged the extracts from the letters he had written to his wife in the form of a journal.

carriages etc were embarking, and make four
sketches. At 12 o'clock (that was Thursday the
12 Novr.) we got on board a private vessel, and
were carried out of Dover harbour by a light
breeze. Our party consisted of Francis, Mr. Webb[1]
and myself ; Dorant, Master of the great Hotel
in Jermyn Street,[2] who being anxious to visit
Paris attended your brother in the quality of
Groom of the Chambers, Hunter the Valet de
Chambre, and Stephen a most active useful servant. Sir John Packington a Worcestershire
Baronet[3] and his brother an invalid crossed with
us taking over their carriage. The breeze which
had apparently promised to carry us over in three
hours after a few languid puffs died away, and in
a dead calm we tided it to within three miles of
Calais, and hoisted lights at the mast head. No
notice was taken of our signals. Francis who did
not relish the idea of being out all night in a
vessel, the cabin of which had been fresh painted,
and the deck of which exposed us to a very cold
atmosphere sent Dorant and the Captain at
10 o'clock in the boat (which was too small to

[1] Francis Webb [1735–1815]. Miscellaneous writer. Educated in Daventry Nonconformist Seminary. Pastor at Honiton ;
Baptist Minister in St. Paul's Alley, London, 1758–66 ; Deputy-
Searcher at Gravesend, 1766–77, and at Poole, 1777 ; Secretary
to the Envoy to Hesse-Cassel, 1786, and to Paris, 1810. Published
pamphlets, verses, and sermons. Mr. Jackson's secretary was
three years older than Lord Cornwallis.

[2] In 1801 there were three first-class hotels in Jermyn Street,
the St. James's, Blake's, and Dorant's.

[3] Sir John Pakington, D.C.L., eighth Baronet [1760–1830].

carry more or it would have carried me) with a
letter to Citizen Mengauld, Commissaire du
Gouvernement, announcing his approach, and requesting him to give such orders as might facilitate
his landing.   The boat was an hour and a half
reaching Calais owing to the strength of the
current.   Dorant repaired immediately to Mengauld's house, and found the Citizen at supper
with his family, his beard an inch long and his
whole appearance dirty and forbidding.   The
character of this man, and his behaviour to some
English who had fallen in his way, led us to expect
many difficulties and an unpleasant reception, but
we were agreably disappointed.   The moment
the Citizen read Francis's letter he started up,
slapped his forehead in anxious agitation about
what he should order first, and sent his people
about in different ways, quickening their diligence
with an assurance that Monsieur Jackson was
" aussi grand que Milord."[1]   While Dorant was
thus engaged, we eat our supper and all the party
turned into bed in the cabin except myself who
wrapped in great coats was slumbering upon the
deck, when I was roused by a fellow tumbling over
me.   Half a dozen more would have done the same
if I had not started up quickly.   They were the
crew of a good-sized French boat into which we
quickly descended and were rowed away to Calais.
At the mouth of the Harbour we ran upon some

[1] The Marquis Cornwallis.

rocky ground, and were several minutes in getting off. On the pier-head were many people with torches who accompanied and lit us up as we rowed along the Harbour. The Pier is of great length ; it appeared to be half a mile. It was a very dark night, and the effect of the torches borne by sailors, women and soldiers, which alternately illuminated the sea and pier, arms and military ornaments, bare heads and white caps, was very singular, and picturesque. At landing we had to climb over two vessels and up a ladder. When safe we were received with the utmost politeness by an officer who said he was proud of the honour which fell to his share of guarding Monsieur le Ministre during his stay in Calais. " Mettez-vous içi, Monsieur," and immediately his men, fine tall fellows in blue regimentals faced with red, and Grenadier caps, formed themselves round us and we marched to the Street where a Coach was in waiting to convey us to the Auberge. We entered it about one o'clock, yet the whole town seemed to be roused. The queer looks of some of the inhabitants who ran to the doors and windows to stare at us as we passed were truly laughable. There were some literally in chemises and nightcaps. As we alighted at the inn[1] the Guard was drawn up, and saluted ; the Drums

[1] Dessein's. For many years one of the best-known hostelries on the Continent. Lawrence Sterne's stay there gave it European celebrity.

COURTYARD OF DESSEIN'S HOTEL, PARIS, WHERE THE MEMBERS OF THE
JACKSON MISSION STAYED, 13–14 NOV. 1807

FROM J. HILL'S CONTEMPORARY AQUATINT

beating. The Officer then told Francis that the Guard would be on duty the whole night and requested him to take the command of it. These French soldiers are very much what they used to be. When they were called up by the orders of the Commissary, they assembled with the greatest good humour in the Inn-yard, formed themselves into squares of eight, and danced cotillons to the sound of their drums till our arrival. We walked up the great staircase of the auberge amidst a profusion of waxlights, and entered a salle à manger. Two black looking officers of the Police with long dark cloaks walked in and with great respect demanded our passports, examined them with great gravity, and entered our names in a Register. An excellent supper of Soup, Fish, and a variety of well dressed dishes was then served, and in an hour's time we retired to bed—alas, not to sleep for the wine Francis sent to the soldiers on guard set their tongues loose and the whole house echoed to their noise.

I rose at eight o'clock on Friday morning the 13th November, but my boots had been taken away so that I could not leave my room, and there was no bell in it. From the door of my apartment I besought the waiters who frequently passed to get me my boots, I wanted to take a walk before breakfast. They answered me very politely " Oui, Monsieur," but did nothing to help me. I then sat down to read and draw for two hours.

At length I darted out of the room and caught another waiter, " Voulez-vous m'apporter de l'eau chaude ? "—" De l'eau chaude Monsieur ? "—" Oui pour me raser "—" Oh Monsieur Je vais chercher un perruquier "—" Non, non, Je n'ai pas besoin d'un perruquier, Je me rase toujours "—" Tres bien Monsieur Je vais chercher de l'eau chaude "—and away he ran as if he would break his neck ; but neither he nor the eau chaude made their appearance. At length in despair I went to Francis, and besought the help of his Excellency. I found him in bed about as badly off for attendance as I was, and we laughed heartily at each other's miseries. He had been called up at five o'clock by a messenger from Lord Cornwallis, and when he had despatched an answer sent his own servants to the waterside with orders not to return without the carriages and baggage. They were not returned, and all the people of the house were so engaged in preparing to do honour to Monsieur le Ministre, that they really never thought of our personal comfort. I then went down to the kitchen and to the great astonishment of a little army of garçons seized and carried off a jug of hot water.

The carriages and baggage arrived soon after, and they had been released and exempted from search by an order from Citizen Mengauld. We had just time to dress and breakfast when the Municipal Officers, and General Ferrand, General of the District waited upon Francis to congratulate

FRENCH TRAVELLING CARRIAGES AT THE BEGINNING OF THE 19TH CENTURY

FROM J. HILL'S CONTEMPORARY AQUATINT

him upon his arrival. They addressed to him a great many elegant compliments which received as many elegant replies. Citizen Mengauld then made his appearance, a man 6 feet 3 inches in height with the countenance and exterior of a fierce Republican. To us however he was exceedingly civil, sat a long time in conversation with Francis, and told him many stories of his humanity to Emigrants and to strangers, whose representations of the Commissary differ materially from the accounts he gives of himself. Pigaud the rich banker, who has amassed an immense fortune since the Revolution came also to visit Francis. He offered his services with great zeal, and indeed performed some of no little use in changing our money and forwarding our heavier luggage. Alas poor Sterne ! I have given you nothing sentimental yet. Alas poor Sterne ! Hadst thou lived to revisit Calais in its present state how would thy feelings have been lacerated on beholding the spot where once stood the Monastery of the Capucins converted into the gardens of a griping usurer. The spirit of thy gentle friend the monk would have risen to pour his complaints into thy bosom, and to mourn with thee the effects of revolutionary madness. Pigaud bought the site and ruins of this Monastery and has converted them into a very pretty-looking residence.

Departure from Calais

About two o'clock an enormous bill was
settled, and the beat of drums announced our
departure from Calais. Shut up in a carriage
I could see very little of the country, and that
little did not raise very favourable ideas of its
beauty. It is in general open, and if not highly
cultivated I saw no waste. Scarcely any wood
is to be seen from the road and the population
seemed to be extremely thin. We scarcely met a
human being. On a hill a few miles from Boulogne
we saw a body of Cavalry drawn up, the Officer of
which after inquiring to whom the carriages belonged politely announced that he had the honor
of being appointed to escort us into Boulogne.
The troop formed a line on each side of the road,
we passed through them and proceeded. It was
quite dark when we entered the town ; a salute
was fired from the batteries ; and every house
we passed was illuminated. Even the Church
was beautifully lighted up, and looked very
pretty. The empressement of some of the inhabitants was so great, that because they had
not a window in which to stick a candle they
stood at their doors with one in each hand. Before the auberge the garrison both horse and foot
were drawn up, and a numerous mob crowded the
streets. After we had alighted the officers of the
Garrison paid their compliments to Francis, and

were followed in a few minutes by the Municipal officers. The Mayor made a set speech, to which Francis gave a very handsome reply. I think he speaks better in French than in English, he is always dignified and gentlemanly, but I suppose he shines with a little additional lustre in the presence of these Republicans.

The British Minister and the Boulogne Fishwives

When these formalities were settled we sat down to an excellent dinner, to which Francis invited the two Officers on guard. One of them had lost an arm, and told us he had fought in 318 battles. Soon after dinner these officers took their leave, but returned very shortly to introduce some ladies who wished also to pay their compliments. A very pretty young woman walked in at the head of about a dozen more all neatly dressed. She bore in her hand an elegant bouquet, and with apparent timidity and an interesting blush began a song expressing the general joy at the return of peace and a wish that the union of the two nations might be eternal. She then desired Francis to accept the bouquet as a token of their respect for him, and their peculiar joy at his arrival. He received the present with all due gallantry, saluted the fair donor on each cheek, assured her of his lively gratitude for her elegant compliment and expressed the peculiar satisfaction with which he bore to this country the amicable sentiments of the English nation. Francis heard afterwards that this was a deputation from the fishwomen,[1] and ordered Hunter to present them with a handsome sum of money, this was instantly declined with an assurance that the manner in which his Excellency had received the compliment was infinitely more valuable. Is it not very curious that we should meet with such a reception at Boulogne, into which place Nelson a few weeks since was pouring death and devastation ?

The same Garde-d'Honneur was continued during the night, and though we left the town at 5 the next morning, the Cavalry attended the carriages, and the batteries saluted our departure. At a little distance from Boulogne a monument was pointed out to me though it was so dark I could not see it erected on the spot where Pilâtre de Rozière the unfortunate aeronaut was killed ; he fell from a great height by the bursting of a balloon.[2] The cavalry attended us two posts, but we were received at Montreuil by some National Guards, resembling in variety of dress, age, and

[1] The Poissardes, the wives and daughters of the fishermen. They are remarkable for their strength and perseverance in loading or unloading the boats, which on account of the shallowness of the coast cannot come up to the beach.—D. W. This scene greatly amused young George Jackson, who, however, calls them *Mesdames les Matelotes.*

[2] Pilâtre de Rozière or Rozier was killed with his companion Romaine near Boulogne on 15 June, 1785.

discipline Falstaff's regiment of ragamuffins. We had here likewise a visit from the Municipality, and after that a good breakfast. We sat in the room which Sterne occupied, and looked out of the window from which he saw and hired La Fleur. Francis received a bouquet here also, but it was presented by a mercenary old woman.

I now changed places with Mr. Webb and accompanied Francis the rest of the journey; Dorant with whom I rode from Calais was a very pleasant companion, as well as exceedingly attentive and respectful. To an Englishman the first appearance of the post horses and drivers is very strange. The horses small with long manes and tails, large heavy saddles, and traces of ropes. The drivers with immense queues and enormous jack-boots, cracking their whips, and talking to the animals all the way; yet they scramble on at a good rate, some posts very rapidly. We saw many national cockades, and heard every now and then the title of Citoyen, but I thought they considered it not respectful to address the epithet to us. The most evident effects of the Revolution were visible in the ruined state of the Churches, and especially of the Monasteries. The former indeed have not suffered so much, and might be easily repaired; the latter have generally little more than fragments of broken walls remaining of their former grandeur. About a league from Abbeville we were met by a body of Chasseurs,

c

the officer of which accosted Francis with the greatest respect, and attended him to the auberge. Some other officers waited on him while the horses were changing, and the Municipality sent to signify their intention of doing the same as soon as they could dress, which enabled him to save them and himself the trouble and the honour. The Chasseurs escorted the carriages two posts (12 miles). The appearance of these men was picturesque and military. Their furniture, accoutrements, arms etc are handsome, especially brass helmets of an antique fashion with long floating horsehair. As Francis was anxious to reach Amiens that night, there was no time to spare and we did not quit the carriages till past ten when we arrived there accompanied by escorts from station to station. We took the people of Amiens by surprise and the lateness of the hour prevented all compliments except what were paid us by the Aubergiste who set before us a very good supper, and then like an unconscionable rogue charged the next morning two guineas a head for eating. Lord Cornwallis had done all in his power to turn the heads of these fellows and set them agog for English guineas. For every thing that was supplied to him or done for him on his way to Paris he paid double, and the higher their extortionate charges, the better he expressed himself pleased. In presents to servants where half crowns would have been handsome he gave rouleaus of

ten guineas. The consequence of this to succeeding
travellers may easily be guessed, and the bills
presented to Francis did in some instances exceed
all bounds.[1] Excepting this at Amiens he paid
them all, thinking a little excess on such an occa
sion allowable, but from this he made a considerable reduction. Our fellow travellers, Sir John
Packington and his brother tired with their day's
journey took leave of us at Amiens[2] and we
proceeded the next morning after an early breakfast. At every post the appearance of our escort
naturally drew round us a crowd of starers, whose
countenances seemed to indicate pleasure at seeing
us, but we were saluted by very few acclamations,
and heard not the cry of " Vive la Republique."
A good woman who keeps the post-house at
St. Juste expressed her joy at seeing the English
by sending an offer to Francis to open her larder
and cellar to him and his attendants free of charge.
The offer was gracefully acknowledged but of
course not accepted.

A little short of Chantilly is a military station
where our escort was to be relieved, but as the

---

[1] According to tradition, diplomatists have apparently always
been regarded as fair game by hotel-keepers, English and foreign
alike. The Duke de Nivernais' bill at the Red Lion Inn, Canter-
bury, after the signing of the Peace of Paris in 1761, has been
immortalized by the Annual Register. He was charged £3 for
wax candles and £2 10s. for broken glass and china.

[2] The Marquis Cornwallis and Mr. Anthony Merry arrived at
Amiens from Paris on 3 Dec., 1801. He had passed through the
city on his way to the French capital on 6 Nov.

orders were sent from place to place we found them at this station not ready. They requested us to wait. Francis was soon tired of this, and having a long hill before us to climb told them he would go on slowly. We had scarcely reached the summit when we heard a loud cry of " Citoyen, Citoyen." On stopping the Serjeant of the Gens d'Armes (a Corps corresponding nearly with our Yeomanry, and who had attended us from the time the Chasseurs left us) rode up to the carriage, and in a surly tone asked Francis if it was necessary to escort him any further. Francis only answered, coolly, " Je suis Ministre de sa Majesté Britannique, et je vous prie de suivre les ordres que vous avez reçus." " Il faut donc suivre votre voiture." " S'il vous plait." We heard a growl as he drew up the window, and guarded by this Republican we proceeded to Chantilly.

Traces of the Revolution

On entering the Auberge which appeared large and handsome I was struck by a total change in the appearance of the house, which was less à l'anglaise than any I had seen. We were shewn into a neat room, the floor of which was laid with glazed sexagonal tiles, in a recess shut off by a curtain stood a bed, and by the side of it a dressing closet. Our supper was not so sumptuous as others had been but it was very acceptable, and while the servant was laying the cloth Francis

asked the young woman who waited several
questions about the magnificent château and
domains of the Montmorency family, which were
a few years since the ornament of the country and
the admiration of travellers. It was a subject
which gave her pain for when he asked her if the
house was in ruins she said " Ah oui, Monsieur,
oui " in so mournful an accent as to be quite
touching. The fine extensive woods were cut down
last winter by an order of Government, and the
estates sold in lots chiefly to the tenants who say
that if the representative of the family were to
return and claim his own they would readily
surrender up the property on receiving leases, so
much do they regret the effects of the Revolution.
A colossal statue in bronze of the great Marshal
Luxembourg whose military talents gave lustre
to the reign of Louis XIV stood over the dome of
the principal stable. When, during the Revolution devastation and plunder were practiced
every where with impunity a number of people
assembled to pull it down. They could not for a
long time accomplish their object. At length they
procured long ropes and forty horses, and drew
the statue from its base. The weight was so great
that it sunk a hole six feet in the ground. There
is something curious and interesting in the history
of the man who before the Revolution enjoyed the
honours and estates of the Montmorency family.
M. Luxembourg was a great favourite and con-

stant attendant on Louis XVI during the few last years of his Reign.[1] He often entreated that unfortunate Monarch to adopt such vigorous and decisive measures as would in all probability restore to the throne of France its antient power and splendour. The day before the fatal 10th of August Luxembourg commanded the Troops 4000 in number which were stationed in the Tuilleries to guard the Royal Family. The Duke de Brissac was second in command. The attack of the National Troops being hourly expected the following plan was arranged and an adherence to it solemnly promised on the part of the King—that if either of these officers should be killed or disabled the King should immediately come forward and take the chief command in person. Early on the 10th the attack commenced, and a desperate conflict was maintained for some hours, till the Duke de Brissac received a ball in his heart. Luxembourg immediately sent for his Aide de Camp to inform his Majesty, and implore him to come out and assume the command. The King was then in a cellar with the Queen and his children clinging round him. His resolution was not equal to the leaving them. He sent answers however by that and subsequent messengers that he was coming

---

[1] Charles Emmanuel Sigismond de Montmorency, Duc de Luxembourg. He is frequently mentioned in *The Diary and Letters of Madame d'Arblay*. Edition of 1904. See Vol. VI, pp. 99, 127, 129, 132, etc. He was the first friend and patron of General d'Arblay, and returned to Paris with Louis XVIII in 1814.

presently. Luxembourg finding that his men began to grow dissatisfied at not seeing the King at their head as had been repeatedly promised them, went himself and said, " If your Majesty does not come out and animate the troops all is lost. Sire, if you are successful you will continue King of France, or even should you fall your son will be instantly proclaimed your successor." The Queen reproached Luxembourg with speaking so freely and said the King should not go into unnecessary danger. In this the irresolute Louis acquiesced. Luxembourg returned to his men and for some time the contest continued when news was brought that the king had fled from the Palace. A consternation instantly seized the troops. All exertion ceased. The National Guards rushed in and massacred every one they could find in the Palace. Luxembourg made his escape at the time they entered by means of a key he had procured the day before for the King's own use in case of necessity ; it opened a private door into the street. He ran into the house of a mercer who had for many years served his family. Two or three of the National troops pursued him closely and he concealed himself in a small closet under the stairs where he overheard the fellows ask a little girl which way he went and she told them he had run through a back door then open. He then disguised himself in things belonging to the mercer's wife and in the night quitted Paris. After undergoing excessive fatigues and hardships he landed at Margate in this disguise without a sixpence in his pocket.

Monsieur Dorant's Story

I have got into a long story before I was aware of it, but will now proceed. I should have introduced it by saying that I had it from my fellow traveller Dorant who was going to Paris to visit this very M. Luxembourg. Some years before, Dorant when in Paris obtained from M. Calonne[1] an order for the removal of two valuable packages with a ticket of exemption. Before he could remove them that Minister's retirement occasioned their being seized and confiscated. Luxembourg actuated only by a desire to do an act of justice procured their restoration to the right owner without knowing who that owner was.

A waiter of Dorant's[2] came to him one morning and said a poor miserable Frenchman had come into the house, and asked for a roll and a little coffee for he was dying with hunger. " Had not I better turn him out, Sir ? " Dorant said he would give him something to eat first ; and because his wife seconded the waiter's proposal he carried the

---

[1] Charles Alexander de Calonne [1734–1802]. For a time his financial schemes promised well, but he was ultimately dismissed by Louis XVI and disgraced. He fled to London. In 1792 he was residing in Piccadilly. Frequent references to him are made in Miss Berry's *Letters and Journal*. See Vol. I, pp. 174, 175, 248, and 259. His *Letter on the State of France, Present and Future* was violently attacked by Earl Stanhope.

[2] At Dorant's Hotel in Jermyn Street.

coffee himself, and instantly recognized his benefactor. Luxembourg had forgotten the obligation
he had conferred, but he accepted the assistance
of his grateful host, who immediately cloathed
him, and advanced him 20 guineas a month for
his support.

By the Laws then existing in France, an
emigrant's wives and children were under sentence
of death, and their property at the disposal of the
Government. When Robespierre passed a Decree
allowing the wives of such persons to divorce
themselves and to marry again, the divorce was
to ensure to them the quiet possession of their
property. Madame Luxembourg, who had before
the Revolution an immense fortune in her own
right was the first who appeared at the Bar of the
Convention to claim the benefit of this Decree,
and during all the subsequent changes of the
Government preserved her wealth by renouncing
her husband. When Luxembourg heard this he
told Dorant that he must endeavour to live upon
less for that he had now no chance of repaying
him. After he had been a few months in England
Mr. Windham[1] sent for him and offered him the
command of a regiment destined for the unfortunate expedition to Quiberon. Luxembourg
declined it, saying that though his services and his

---

[1] William Windham [1750–1810]. Secretary for War, with
seat in the Cabinet under Pitt, 1794–1801. The most bitter and
persistent opponent of the Peace of 1801–2.

life were devoted to his King, yet he would never draw his sword against his country under the command of any other power. He told this to Dorant, adding that he could no longer remain in England, because he would not incur the disgrace of being sent out of it under the operation of the Alien Act. He therefore went to Flanders, and continued to receive an allowance from Dorant till his name was struck out of the list of emigrants. He then returned to Paris, where he was well received by his wife, with whom and his two daughters he is now living. He repaid Dorant with interest, and Madame Luxembourg as an expression of her gratitude offered to take his youngest daughter to educate, whom Dorant had contrived to get over to Paris. You may therefore well suppose how extremely anxious my fellow traveller was to see his daughter and his friend. But he was unable to get a Passport ; he therefore engaged himself *nominally* as premier valet de Chambre to Francis, and forms part of his suite, and in that capacity has really been useful and active. I can finish this story, for Dorant has just been with me. On his arrival in Paris he hastened to M. Luxembourg, and found him living in great style in one of the most magnificent Hotels, with all the splendour and state of the old times ; and nothing could exceed the cordiality of his reception. " But " added Dorant " I am sorry I have sent my daughter to them, the style of her education and habits of living will unfit her for the private sphere of her father's family."

Arrival of the Jackson Mission in Paris

This has been a long but I hope not an uninteresting digression. Francis on our arrival at Chantilly sent off Hunter to Paris with the dispatches for Lord Cornwallis, and a letter to Mr. Merry[1]; and ordered him to meet us the next morning at St. Denis. After breakfast on Monday we proceeded towards Paris, but were a little surprized to find by Merry's reply that it was hardly possible to procure accommodation, the place was so full. We went first to his Hotel, and after waiting some time drove to the Hotel de la Grange Battaillieres,[2] which being almost wholly

[1] Antony Merry, d. 14 June, 1835; m. 21 Jan., 1803, the widow of John Leather of Herringford Hall. Minister in France, the United States, Denmark, and Sweden from April, 1802, to April, 1809. Dr. J. Holland Rose speaks of him as an abler diplomatist than Lord Cornwallis.

[2] The Hôtel de la Grange Batelière is also known as the Hôtel Pujol or Pujot, from the name of its owner. In 1801 it stood in the Rue Pinon, Quartier Mont Blanc, close to the Boulevard Italian. In the *Almanach National* of 1801 the Hôtel de la Grange Batelière is given as the residence of the American plenipotentiaries Messrs. Davis and Ellsworth. Adjoining it was the Hotel D'Oigny, the scene of the "bals des victimes" after the Terror and many brilliant dances during the Consulate. The Rue Pinon was absorbed by the still existing Rue de la Grange Batelière. The site of the hotel which so long bore that name is now occupied by the celebrated auction-rooms known as the Hôtel Druot. Four days later Mr. George Jackson, who speaks of the hotel as the Hotel Pajol, made the following note in his diary : " My brother, for the present, pur-

occupied by Lord Cornwallis and his Suite, left us apartments not quite suited to the dignity of the Mission. My room is however very comfortable, and I am now sitting in it by a good fire. Wood is the only fuel here, but it is much pleasanter than coals, except the chimney should smoke.

I think I have now given you a complete detail of our journey, which was rendered very pleasant not only by all the circumstances I have described but likewise by the great good humour and attention of Francis. I look forward to the passing my time in Paris very much to my satisfaction, considering what I have given up in quitting for a time the society of my dear wife. I shall now commence a daily journal of all I see and hear. As your amusement is my chief object, your thanks will be my best reward. If you derive half the pleasure in receiving which I shall do in communicating my observations, I shall not consider my time to be misemployed.

posely keeps in the background, for Lord C. is a little sore at his arrival in Paris—being an independent envoy, before he and his party have left it. He does not wish to ruffle the good old gentleman's feelings, nor will he allow him to know, lest it should further annoy him that, M. Talleyrand has taken advantage of his exceedingly small acquaintance with the French language to declare himself to have been at a loss to understand the distinct nature of my brother's functions, as attempted to be explained to him by his lordship. . . . My brother cannot have his audience of the First Consul until he receives his letters of credence, which have been delayed on account of some hesitation here—on the part of M. Talleyrand it is supposed—in forwarding similar credentials to M. Otto."

. . . Be assured that amid all the attractions of
novelty I shall never for a moment cease to be
Your own
D. W.

Nov. 16, 1801–24 Brumaire, Year 10.

We arrived in Paris about one oclock, and after
some difficulty were lodged in small apartments
in the Hotel de la Grange Battaillieres. Dined
together at 6, drew upon our own resources for
amusement, and separated early.

Nov. 17.

Our breakfast is fixed at nine. I accompanied
Francis in his carriage to make visits, and deliver
letters of introduction. The facility with which
Frenchmen hung their fellow countrymen during
the revolutionary changes of their Government
was owing to their lamps being suspended in the
middle of their streets by a small cord. When the
cry of " à la lanterne " followed any unfortunate
object of their political hatred, they had only to
lower a lamp and suspend him in its place, for the
halter was ready to their hands. The reply of
Beaumarchais to some rabble who called out for
his suspension " à la lanterne," saved his life.
" À la lanterne ! Quand même vous me mettriez
à la lanterne, vous n'en verriez pas plus clairs."
They laughed at his wit, gave him three cheers,
and set him at liberty.

Francis drove to the different Ministers, and

seemed very well pleased with their reception of him. He was invited to dinner the following day by Decrès, Minister of the Marine.[1] We were admitted by Madame Decrès in her bedroom. The bed was as ornamental as magnificent draperies would make it. There were two men sitting with her who affected to be à l'anglaise with dirty boots, cropped heads and large whiskers. I find it is a prevailing notion that all the English dress in that manner. There was nothing particular to admire in the external appearance of their public offices, and I had time to study them as I sat in the carriage during Francis's visits. In all the court-yards were planted Trees of Liberty. The air of Paris seems not to agree with them. I saw not one of a flourishing appearance, and some were quite dead. On his return home Francis found an appointment from Citizen Talleyrand, Minister of Foreign Affairs, he accordingly dressed and drove there[2] as quick as possible. He came back in excellent spirits.

[1] Rear-Admiral Denis Decrès [1761-1820], Minister of Marine in 1801. He is celebrated for his heroic defence of the *Guillaume Tell* against the *Foudroyant*, the *Lion*, and the *Penelope* on 30 March, 1800. The *Guillaume Tell*, as the *Malta*, became the largest two-decker in the British Navy except the *Tonnant*.

[2] Talleyrand was then residing in the Rue du Bac in the Faubourg St. Germain.

Mr. Hill joins the Jackson Mission as Secretary

Mr. Hill a Nephew of Sir Richard Hill[1] whom Francis expected to assist him as Secretary arrived to-day. He is an agreeable young man, and promises to be a pleasant addition to our party. Frank Moore told me to-day that I should be heartily sick of Paris in a week, and Col. Pollen represented the morals of the place to be remarkably bad ; there is hardly a modest woman in Paris. When Lord Cornwallis and his suite dined at Talleyrand's they met eleven kept women, and his Lordship had to hand to the diningroom Madame Le Grand[2] the chère amie of the Minister.

[1] Sir Richard Hill, second Baronet [1732–1808]. M.P. for Shropshire, 1780–1806. Hill championed the cause of the Methodist undergraduates expelled from the University of Oxford.

[2] Madame Grand [1762–1835], née Catherine Noël Worlée. Born at Tranquebar in India, and the daughter of a French officer stationed at Pondicherry. In 1777 she became the wife of George Francis Grand or Grant, a clerk in the Indian Civil Service. An intrigue with Sir Philip Francis led to a duel between Grand and the Member of Council, who in his diary for 24 Nov., 1778, had written the words *Omnia vincit amor*, adding cynically on 8 Dec. : " At night, the diable à quatre at the house of G. F. Grant [*sic*], Esqr." From 1782 Madame Grand led an immoral life in Paris, where Madame Vigée Lebrun painted her portrait. From 1798 her name was linked with that of Talleyrand. Their relations were not legalized until 9–10 Sep., 1802, when they were married at the *mairie* of the 10th Arrondissement of Paris. Bonaparte and Josephine, the Consuls Cambacérès and Lebrun, the Secretary of State Maret and others signed the nuptial contract. A very interesting account of the Talleyrands, husband and wife, will be found in Mr. A. d'Alberti's translation of Bernard de Lacombe's *La Vie Privée de Talleyrand* (London, 1910).

A sad state of morals this ! What must such depravity lead to ?—

Nov. 18.

Great pains have been taken to find an Hotel but hitherto unsuccessfully. We shall probably remain where we are till Mr. Merry goes to Amiens with Lord Cornwallis and leaves us his. I walked with Francis and Hill to look at one, but it suited not. Hill and I left him and took a long walk. The streets of Paris are narrow and dirty. Having no pavement for the accomodation of foot passengers they are miserably inconvenient for walking. We went through the gardens of the Tuileries and crossed them in various directions. They are magnificent but all laid out in straight walks and angles. In one corner is a statue of Voltaire miserably executed, enclosed by a high open paling, the area within which is a flower garden. A paper on a board within this paling presents to the lounging spectator a long eulogy on the Philosopher of Ferney, and calls on every one both in prose and verse to do homage to his name.

The British Diplomatists meet at Dinner

Francis dined at Decrès', and came home very well pleased with his visit. He had met all the Ministers of State, and several of the great Generals of the Republic. Moreau, whom he called a most gentlemanly man ; Berthier, pretty well ;

GENERAL PASS GRANTED TO REV. DAWSON WARREN, SIGNED BY CHARLES MAURICE TALLEYRAND, MINISTER OF FOREIGN AFFAIRS, NOV. 1801

Massena, looking like a savage ; Joseph Bonaparte with whom he conversed pleasantly, and
many others beside the British Ambassador
[Cornwallis] and his suite.

We received today our Billets or rather *Cartes
de Sureté*[1] by which we may go any where without
fear of being molested. It is a card of the size
and shape I have drawn but elegantly engraved,
therefore the greatest resemblance I was able to
effect was the ugly writing of Talleyrand.

Honesty and Dishonesty

A singular proof that political fury and not
petty plunder instigated the Parisian populace
during their troubles was mentioned by Col.
Pollen. The Prince de Monaco quitted Paris
abruptly in the beginning of the Revolution, and
left his Hotel, one of the most magnificent in the
City, having only locked up the door. He went
to England where he married a Miss Doyle, and
on his return after ten years' absence found every
thing exactly as he had left it, even the remains
of a breakfast on the table.

[1] *Carte de Sureté.* It is tinted with the three national colours.
It has on one side the Genius of the French Republic, holding in
her left hand an antique rudder and in her right an olive branch
with which she points to an altar of friendship. The reverse
contains the name of the bearer and the signature of Talleyrand,
the Minister for Foreign Affairs. These cards protect those who
carry them from the questions of sentinels and police officers, and
give admission to all museums and public collections. They are
delivered to Ambassadors, Ministers and their suites. Tickets
of a less elegant design are given to other strangers.—D. W.

Nov. 19.

After the instance I have just given you of the honesty of Paris it is rather curious that I should have thus immediately to record Mr. Webb's loss. His watch was stolen this morning. He left the key in his bedroom door. Somebody slipt in and carried it off.

I took a walk with Hill, but the streets are so miserable for pedestrians that I think I shall give it up. We looked into a Panorama of Paris, and another of Toulon, both wretched things after Barker's.[1]

Francis dined with the Spanish Ambassador, M. Le Chevalier de Azara and met the same party he was with yesterday. He came home early and changed his full dress for a frock coat to go to the opera.

His Consular Majesty (for so I may call Bonaparte in consequence of the regal state he is gradually assuming) dwells awfully retired from the public eye. He only appears in public upon grand parade days, and then surrounded by some of his finest guards. So I stand little chance of seeing him this month. Even Lord Cornwallis has only had one private audience, for Bonaparte gives no dinners and sees no company.[2]

[1] The famous panorama in Leicester Square.
[2] On 9 Nov. Lord Cornwallis wrote to Major-General Ross that he was uncertain as to whether Bonaparte intended to grant him a private interview. On the following day, however, he reports to Lord Hawkesbury that the audience had taken place :

THE PONT NEUF, PARIS 1801-2

FROM AN AQUATINT BY J. HILL

THE TUILERIES IN 1801–2

FROM A CONTEMPORARY AQUATINT BY J. HILL

assumed the Government of the Republic, chiefly
extracted from the Official Journals. Another
purchase I made was of a book better known and
written in a most elegant and entertaining manner
*Précis Historique de la Révolution Française, par
Rabaut de St. Etienne.* He was an eye witness and
no inconsiderable actor in the scenes he describes,
and he was one of the many victims sacrificed in
consequence of them. A continuation of the work
by Lacretelle brings the History down to the end
of 1792.

A Second Visit to the Louvre

My visit yesterday with Francis to the " Musée
central des Arts " highly gratifying as it was, was
only a taste of a feast which I knew I should enjoy
better by myself. I have not got a sufficient stock
of epithets to convince others I am pleased. I told
you that in the lower apartments are placed the
works of ancient sculptors, above, are those of the
painters. A few of the statues were from the
collections of the late King or of his nobles, but
the greater part were gained by the French army
in Italy. The treaty of Tolentino empowered
their Government to send six commissioners to
choose from the Capitol and the Vatican the finest
specimens of sculpture preserved there. There
can be no doubt of the judgment with which the
selection was made, nor were care and expence
spared in transporting them to Paris. The arrival
of this valuable collection was attended with

public rejoicings and celebrated with feasts of triumph. Men of the first taste and abilities were employed to arrange them, and the establishment was taken under the immediate care of the Government under the Department of the Minister of the Interior. I must take care and not to tell my stories twice over, though I think I could come here a hundred times with fresh interest. I was particularly struck today in La Salle des Saisons with a beautiful statue of Venus coming out of the bath—and another, of exquisite grace and elegance representing Cupid in the act of stringing his bow. In La Salle des Romains my attention was rivetted by the Dying Gladiator and the Antinous of the Capitol. I also peeped between the boards and saw a little more of the Laocoon which is thought to be the most perfect work ever executed by the chisel. This celebrated piece of sculpture was discovered at Rome in 1506 among the ruins of a Palace which had belonged to Titus. Pliny who had seen it speaks of it with admiration and records the names of the three sculptors who united their talents to produce it, Agesander, Polydorus and Athenodorus. At least so Mr. Webb tells me. I must look it out when I get home. The group is formed of five blocks of marble, Pliny says but of one. It follows that this object of our admiration is a copy of the blocks most skilfully joined. The right arm of the father, and two of the arms of the sons are wanting.

Inauguration of the Statue of Apollo

I visited again that noblest of statues the Apollo. My vocabulary is exhausted. So I will descend to historical facts. On the 16th Brumaire in the year 9 of the Republic,[1] the First Consul accompanied by the Consul Le Brun, and the Counseller of State Benezech performed with great pomp the inauguration of Apollo. An inscription was then placed on the pedestal stating that it had been found at Antium about the close of the 15th century, placed in the Vatican by Pope Julius II in the beginning of the 16th, was gained by the Italian Army under the orders of General Bonaparte in the 5th year of the Republic and placed here on the 21st of Germinal year 8 in the first year of his Consulate.[2] This statue is placed at the upper end of the room within a space railed off. There are some beautiful collumns taken from one of their churches near it. And on each side is a fine statue of Venus. One of these that of the Capitol is considered one of the most perfect as well as most beautiful of the antient statues.

No description of this wonderful collection can convey an adequate idea of it. To visit it must be the finest treat in the world. The apartments in which it is arranged are admirably adapted to the purpose except in some few instances where

[1] Friday, 7 Nov., 1800.
[2] Friday, 11 April, 1800.

the light does not fall favourably. The ceilings are well painted and richly gilt, and the flooring inlaid with various coloured marbles.

I did not say that the weather this morning was excessively bad. Francis kindly took Hill and myself in the chariot to the Museum and soon left us there. After lingering some time among the statues we ascended to the first floor by a handsome staircase on the landings of which are a few specimens of modern sculpture. The first room contained the Productions of living French Artists. Here and there appeared a work of merit but it was among a great deal of rubbish. No doubt the opportunities of studying the finest models now brought within the reach of these painters will occasion great improvement. Some sculpture, engravings, and architectural designs are likewise exhibited. We proceeded to the Grand Gallery which indeed well deserves that name being 1600 feet in length. A small portion at the farther end is partitioned off. The walls are covered with the finest productions of the French, Flemish and Italian schools. It is much to be regretted that the light being admitted through windows occasions one side of the gallery to be in darkness while the other has all the glare of reflection, so that but few of the pictures can be seen to advantage. The inconvenience is much increased by the high varnishing they have received, which it is to be hoped will not prove hereafter injurious to the colouring. We prevailed upon one of the attendants to admit us behind the partition that we might see the celebrated Transfiguration of Raphael. He said there were objections to the shewing it in its present state as it was not yet varnished. I thought it in a better state for inspection than any picture in the Gallery. I will not attempt to particularize any of the Paintings but bring you home a catalogue, though that will not help you much. You must see them. The bad light allowed me to feel an increased regret that many of them have been torn from the places they have long been the admiration of the world to be fixed where much of their merit is lost by being too near the eye or in other respects unfavorably situated. The Museum being open today to the Public a great croud of ragamuffin citizens male and female were walking about and criticizing. Though their appearance was against them they were very orderly. But I should think that Modesty if she were ever an inhabitant of Paris would be improved by promiscuous crowds of both sexes staring at these unveiled representations of nature. One figure attracted my attention, a young man with hair plaited up and dressed a la grecque, in pantaloons and half-boots. I whispered to Hill to observe his effeminacy. He told me it was a woman. I doubted the possibility of such effrontery. We passed her again and were convinced. This boldfaced impudence they tell me is not at all uncommon and laugh at my delicacy fresh from London.

Francis took me in the evening to the Théâtre de Molière[1] but instead of one of that writer's comedies they gave us a tragedy of Voltaire of which I understood only every tenth sentence and consequently found it dull enough. The rhimes were to my ears unnatural and unpleasant. It is a pretty Theatre but no musick and no change of scene. The curtain let down at the close was very rich. A head of Apollo with rays of light issuing from it and illuminating a magnificent border.

A Stroll with my French Professor

Nov. 22.

Les canons annoncèrent de bonne heure ce matin la rentrée du Corps Legislatif.

C'est aujoudhui Dimanche, et J'avois oublié le jour quand je m'arrangeai avec Monsr. (dont le nom m'est à present inconnu, mais qui par l'introduction du M. Pougens entreprend m'enseigner la langue) de venir à dix heures. Quand il arriva je lui fis me excuses, et il eut la bonté de me proposes de me faire voire les Eglises principales de cette Ville. C'etoit une offre trop intéressante pour être refusée, et nous allâmes ensemble. Il me

---

[1] The usual name for the Comédie Française. It was a vast building with a Doric colonnade. There is an engraving of it about this time by Blanchard *ainé* after a drawing by Courvoisier.

conduisit d'abord par le Palais Egalité çidevant Royal, qui etait la residence ordinaire du Duc D'Orléans. De là nous fumes a la halle au blé, une rotonde superbe, hardie, et qui merite d'être vue. Elle est battie sur le terrain de l'ancien Hôtel des Comtes de Soissons. Les sacs de farine qui y etaient arrangés parurent m'assurer qu'il n'y-a point de famine ici, neanmoins le pain est du même prix comme chez nous. Après cela notre objet etait d'aller a l'Eglise de St. Eustache. Elle est tres belle, et d'un architecture Gothique, mais ma memoire ne m'en rappelle les details, parceque j'etais tres attentif à profiter de la conversation de mon bon instructeur, a l'honnêteté et aux manières obligeantes duquel je ne puis donner trop de louanges. Nous traversâmes le Pont Neuf où était autrefois la statue d'Henri IV que le Populace mit à bas dans le commencement de la Révolution à peu près deux ans auparavant cette même populace forçait les passants de lui ôter leur chapeaux. There I should have written five times as much in English, and I return with pleasure to my own language. My walk lasted three hours, in which time I visited the churches of Notre Dame and St. Sulpice. They were all empty, deserted and miserable. Once or twice I saw a poor person kneeling, and it seemed just to remind me that God was not universally forgotten.

A funeral as I apprehend of a poor man passed us in the street. The coffin covered with black

cloth was carried in an open hearse and followed
by an officer of Police on foot, whose duty it is to
see that the bodies of the deceased are carried to
the cemeteries, enclosures out of the City where
no distinctions are allowed except a common
wooden cross, and where no religious service is
performed.   They have recently relaxed a little
in this point, at least the attendance of a Priest
has passed without notice ; but it is by stealth,
and no permission whatever is given to erect a
Monument.

I passed by the ruins of a Church dedicated to
St. André des Arcs.   It was melancholy to see in
a country which not long since was called Christian, workmen pulling down upon a Christian
Sabbath a Christian place of worship.   There
were only a few arches remaining.

On arriving at the Palais du Corps Legislatif I
endeavoured to go in but the crowd was so great
as to render it impossible.   Some of their Ministers
went in state attended by horse-guards.   So much
for equality and fraternity etc.   As I was looking
at one of them with my little opera glass a sentinel spoke to me as I thought in a very insolent
manner, and I took no notice of it.   He spoke a
second time and with still more violence, but I
did not understand him.   My conductor told him
I was a stranger and took me out of the croud ;
he then explained that I had been guilty of dis-
respect to the dignity of a minister by looking at

him through an opera glass. Knowing my way home I dismissed M. Le Gros, first offering him a Louis as a compliment. He refused it. I explained to him that entrance money was common in England but he persisted in his refusal, saying that at the end of the month he would give me his account the payment of which would be all the remuneration he should think of.

[While the unpaid chaplain was walking with his tutor the unpaid attaché was witnessing one of the reviews which entered so largely into the life of the first Consul. His impressions both of the ceremonial and the central figure in it are very interesting. " I have heard some English officers say," he wrote next day to his mother at Bath, " that these parades are not nearly so well conducted[1] as some far less pretentious ones in England ; but I do know, that the parade of this Republic General was a right royal one, and on a small scale, an unrivalled display of the pomp and circumstance of war ? I was much struck by the personal appearance of Bonaparte, for the caricatures, and the descriptions which the English papers delight to give of him, prepare one to see a miserable pigmy ; hollow-eyed, yellow-skinned, lantern-jawed, with a quantity of lank hair, and a nose of enormous proportions. But, though of low stature—perhaps five feet five or six—his

[1] *Diaries and Letters of Sir George Jackson*, Vol. I, p. 19.

figure is well proportioned, his features are hand-some, complexion rather sallow, hair very dark, cut short and without powder. He has fine eyes, full of spirit and intelligence, a firm severe mouth, indicating a stern and inflexible will, in a word, you see in his countenance, the master-mind ; in his bearing, the man born to rule. At present the three Consuls reside in the palace, but *on dit*, that Bonaparte finds this arrangement *très gênant ;* that he wants a house to himself, and that numbers two and three will most likely soon be ousted, to accommodate him. Then—but this is only whispered— that large flaunting inscription on the central pavilion of the palace, *République Française* may vanish, as well as the republican clock which stands above it, with the border divided into ten instead of twelve parts."]

Nov. 23.

After my lesson I passed the morning in the Museum. It is now open only to strangers and artists, and consequently much more pleasant.

A Dinner at Perrégaux's

At ½ past 5 Francis took me to dine with Per-régaux the great banker.[1] Lord Cornwallis and

---

[1] Jean Frederic Perrégaux, Senator and President of the Bank at Paris. A native of Neuchâtel, Switzerland. He was much favoured by Napoleon, but enjoyed the confidence and friendship of Georgina and Elizabeth, Duchesses of Devonshire, and other English women of fashion. He lived at a splendid house in the Rue du Mont Blanc, formerly called the Chaussée d'Antin. It

his Suite, three ladies, an Englishman or two and
a few Frenchmen composed a party of twenty
five. The dinner consisted of two handsome
courses set round a large plateau ornamented with
flowers and biscuit figures. A dessert of fruits and
confectionery in all shapes and devices followed,
forming a chain of fifty or sixty dishes round the
table. Very little wine was drank. The party
retired from the dining room very early, the
gentlemen accompanied the ladies into the drawing room. Ices were handed round, then coffee,
and afterward liqueurs. The entertainment was
shewy and handsome, and the house was superbly
fitted up. Rich painting and gilding with many
large mirrors decorated the walls. One thing
offended me much, the dress of the French women.
Lady Cahir[1] was the only one decent, the costume
of French ladies in the evening is strikingly the
reverse. I sat next a lady who seemed to have
nothing more on than a chemise and a gown and
even these left the whole bust exposed. She
seemed to be of some consequence from the attentions paid her, though we none of us made out
her name. I often start a subject in conversation
because I happen to have French expressions

was originally built by the Prince de Soubise for the famous
dancer Marie Madeleine Guimard, and was variously known as
the Pavilion Guimard or the Temple of Terpsichore. She lived
until 1816.

[1] Lady Cahir, afterwards Countess of Glengall, is frequently
mentioned by Mary Berry. A year or so later she took part in
the private theatricals given by Lord and Lady Abercorn.

E

adapted to it fresh in my memory. I had been
reading about horsemanship, so I asked my neighbour if she was fond of riding, to which she answered by such a history of her confinements and
her nursery, which had deprived her of that
pleasure, that I sat much distressed for a quarter
of an hour, and got heartily laughed at by my
companions afterwards. The rooms are very warm
from the stoves and the women wrap themselves
well in shawls before they go out, or I should
wonder how their health could stand such exposure to the cold. But the effect this fashion
must have on the morals of the country it is
fearful to reflect upon. How can fathers and
Husbands allow it ? How can women themselves
suppose it increases their influence ? They say
Madame Bonaparte discountenances it.

My Talk to Lord Cornwallis

Francis introduced me particularly to Lord
Cornwallis. I thought he would have remembered
my father in America, but his Lordship's memory
did not seem very clear on the subject. Had I
taken them with me to Paris, I could have shewn
him acknowledgments in his own handwriting of
the services my father rendered to the British
Army in Philadelphia.

Joseph Bonaparte was one of this party, Francis
introduced me to him particularly, and he conversed with me a few minutes very pleasantly.

I doubt not that if my knowledge of the language improves I shall get on very well ; I assure you I take pains.

Nov. 24th.

A very unfavorable morning gave me both time and inclination to take a three hours' French lesson. The constantly talking English in our domestic circle is against me.

Francis took me in the carriage to visit Joseph Bonaparte, and Madame Santa Cruz[1] neither at home ; for the former I left my card. In the evening Francis, Hill and myself went to the Théâtre Français, and heard part of the tragedy of Alzine. The ranting and violent gesticulation of the Actors were not at all to my taste. This theatre is fixed up in imitation of the antique style but large pillars of the Tuscan order look heavy and interrupt the sight.

A French Criminal Court

Nov. 25th.

Having engaged Le Gros my French Master to

---

[1] Mentioned in the *Mémoires de la Duchesse d'Abrantès* (Vol. V, p. 278) as " la Marquise de Santa Crux, charmante et aimable femme." Her husband, M. de Santa Crux, was a Spanish Grandee of the First Class, who for a time attached himself to the fortunes of Joseph Bonaparte, and accepted the post of Chamberlain, but afterwards joined the Nationalists. It is just possible, however, that the lady visited by Mr. Jackson and his chaplain was Madame de Santa Croce, an Italian princess of ancient lineage, who in 1801–2 frequented the principal Paris salons, and is spoken of by Miss Berry as *aussi de colletée que les Francaises.*

conduct me this morning to the Courts of Criminal
Justice, Hill and I went with him immediately
after breakfast. We were disappointed for the
Court was not sitting. We went to another which
is a Court of Appeal from inferior jurisdictions.
This was engaged in an interesting cause. A
widow brought her complaint against her husband's
brother for withholding from her considerable
property, and refusing her the care of her children.
She had lost her cause in another court, but here
was successful. The Counsel who was speaking
when we entered was the most violent orator I
have ever heard. He threw himself into the
strangest attitudes, clapped his hands, smote the
desk before him with his clenched fists, and
foamed like a madman as he roared out an enumer-
ation of the unjust acts. In the last great ebulli-
tion he seemed to clap, stamp, kick, and roar all
at once—" Voilà qu'il a volé—L'infame " and
sunk down exhausted. Yet he was eloquent and
interested me much in the widow's favour. The
Court consisted of seven Judges.

1. The President.
2. The 6 other Judges.
3. The advocates for Plaintiffs.
4. The advocates for Defendants.
5. The Commissaire du Government, who
when the lawyers had finished their pleadings,
rose and summed up the case. The Judges retired
into another Chamber to determine on their sen-

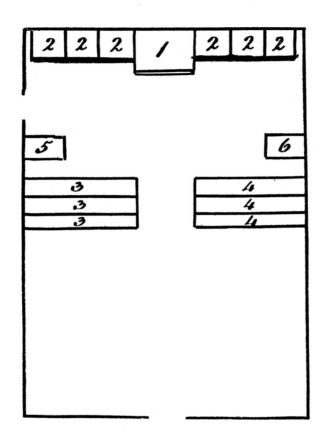

COURT

in the

PALAIS de JUSTICE.

tence. On their return the President delivered their decision standing. Then

6. The Clerk of the Court entered it in a Register.

It is presumptuous in me to give an opinion upon any thing, having so little knowledge of the language, I therefore speak with hesitation. They appeared to decide upon the common principles of Justice, and not according to the directions of existing Laws. The People consider themselves to be in great want of a Code of Civil Law. The present Government assures the Nation that it shall be an object of their early and anxious attention to supply this deficiency.[1] Amidst the convulsions of the Revolution many Laws were enacted of so iniquitous a nature that when recorded in History they will scarcely be credited. Mr. Shaw, an American whom I have seen two or three times, pointed out one of the laws which is still in force. The law of presuccession. Previous Laws had declared the estates and goods of emigrants to be national property and at the disposal of Government. The Law of presuccession went still farther, and, supposing all emigrants to possess an Interest or vested right in property which had not yet come into their possession but

---

[1] The Civil Code became law in 1804. After undergoing some slight modifications and additions it was, in 1807, renamed the Code Napoléon. Its provisions were adopted in Italy in 1806. Dr. J. Holland Rose (*Life of Napoleon*, Vol. I, p. 287) speaks of it as a work " of almost pyramidal solidity."

might do so in the course of nature, compelled
the fathers and grandfathers and other relations
of such persons to deliver up to the State whatever portions of their property might accrue to
them in the light of heirs at law. A particular
instance of the operation of this Law has lately
happened. An old lady had her estate seized,
and was compelled to pay one third of its value
before it was restored to her, because the name of
one of her three grandsons was inserted in the list
of emigrants.

At the return of Emigrants when their names
were duly erased from the lists of proscription, it
was at first usual to restore to them such parts of
their property as might remain in the hands of
Government particularly forest lands which were
never sold but called National Domains. An
edict has passed within the last six months to
stop all restitution.

Frenchmen seem to have no idea of the nature
either of Liberty or of Justice, that is of their real
principles. One of them who considered such laws
as I have just mentioned as nothing extraordinary
or unreasonable, was struck with horror at the
sight of the stamp in my hat, for which as I told
him, I had been compelled to pay two shillings ;
and he exclaimed with great vehemence " Ou est
votre Liberté tant vantée ? " His indignation
must have proceeded from some misapprehension
which I could not rectify, for my explanation that

GARDEN FRONT OF THE HÔTEL CARAMAN, RUE ST. DOMINIQUE, PARIS,
IN THE WINTER OF 1801-2

the English People laid that tax upon themselves by their own representatives in Parliament did not satisfy him in the least, but he congratulated himself upon living in a land of Freedom and Justice.

After hearing the conclusion of the Widow's Trial we went into the Hall where the unfortunate Queen of France Marie Antoinette was arraigned and condemned. A Statue of the Genius of the Republic with a spear and Cap of Liberty is placed at one end, while seats for the Judges and Benches for the Counsel etc occupy the other. This is now used as the Court of Criminal Justice. The Palais de Justice is a handsome Building, formerly a Royal Palace, but had been used for a long time either by the Parliaments of Paris or by some of the Public Offices. A fine old Chapel which stood near it is now almost demolished. In a triangular space near the Palais de Justice they are erecting a Monument to General Desaix.[1]

Francis has settled to take Mr. Merry's apartment on Lord Cornwallis's departure for Amiens. The Hotel belonged to M. le Marquis de Caraman, who with three sons and five daughters and some of their husbands and wives lived in it before the Revolution. The Revolution ruined them as it

[1] General Louis Charles Antoine Desaix de Veygoux [1768–1800]. Desaix was one of Napoleon's most devoted lieutenants. He was taken prisoner by Admiral Keith 3 March, 1800, and was killed some three months later at the battle of Marengo (14 June, 1800). He fell on the same day and at the same hour that Kléber was assassinated in Egypt. The Desaix monument is also mentioned by Miss Berry (*Letters and Journal*, Vol. III, p. 171).

did thousands, and their chief subsistence is now derived from letting it.

There is great reason to suppose that when the Pope and the first Consul shall have settled the Religion of the State, the present French Calendar will be abolished, and the Christian era restored.[1]

The British Minister Dines with Fouché

Nov. 26.

N.I.P. you used to write when you had *N*othing *I*n *P*articular to record in your Diary. These letters will pretty nearly tell the history of today ; except that I took a walk with Francis to call on Mr. Short (not Shaw) the American. He is full of information and exceedingly agreeable to all the party.

Francis dined today with Fouché[2] the Minister of Police. This man was celebrated during the Revolution for carrying into full effect the sanguinary Decrees of the Convention. He was one of the Judges who at the condemnation of the mild and humane Louis said " La Mort." He had the infernal distinction of inventing what he called

---

[1] The Concordat between Napoleon and Pius VII was signed at Paris on 15 July, 1801. The Revolutionary Calendar existed from 1793 until 31 Dec., 1805 (10 Nivose, Year XIV), when the Gregorian mode of calculation was restored by Napoleon.

[2] Joseph Fouché, afterwards Duc d'Otranto [1763–1820]. Became Minister of Police in 1799. He married in 1815 a lady belonging to the family of Castellane. He was exiled in 1816, and died at Trieste in 1820. In November, 1801, Fouché was on the Quai Malaquai which still exists.

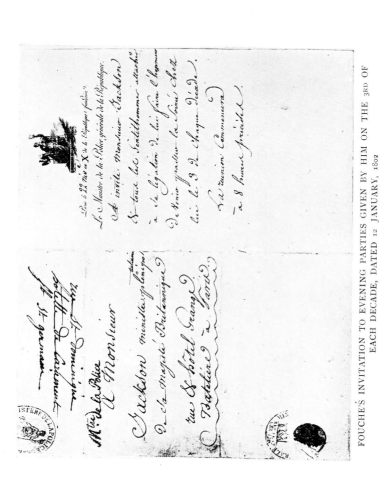

FOUCHÉ'S INVITATION TO EVENING PARTIES GIVEN BY HIM ON THE 3RD OF
EACH DECADE, DATED 12 JANUARY, 1802

" Revolutionary marriages " by tying a man and a woman together and flinging them into the water. When he found the work of death too tedious while he dispatched his victims singly, he slaughtered them by hundreds in his noyades and fusillades. Few were so active as Fouché in these scenes of horror, yet he now lives in luxury and splendour. Francis says his house is the most magnificent he has yet seen in Paris.

French Marriages

Nov. 27th.

I asked my French Master this morning some questions respecting the present forms of marriage. He began in a most methodical manner and I requested the favour of him to begin again and allow me to write from his dictation. " En France," said my worthy instructor, " En France jusqu'à présent voici l'usage relatif au Marriage. Lorsque les jeunes gens so plaisent mutuellement, et que des Pères et des Mères sont d'accord, on passe un contrat devant un Notaire. Dans se contrat les Parens conviennent entre eux de se qu'ils veulent donner reciproquement a leur enfants. Ensuite on fait publications dans les Arrondissemens du futur et de la future. Ensuite le jour du Mariage arrivé, et les Parens assemblés (ou d'après la nouvelle coutume simplement les Pères et les Mères, s'il y en a) et quatre temoins, ils se transportent a l'arrondissement dans lequel demeure la Mariée, et la en presence du Maire ou de son substitut de Mariage est prononcé au Nom de la Loi dans la maniere suivante. L'Officier public commence par appeler de Mari le premier et lui dit. 'M.— Citoyen, vous consentez à prendre pour legitime et future épouse Mademoiselle N.— ici presente, à lui garder la foi et la fidelité conjugale.' L'époux ayant repondu, 'Oui, Citoyen,' l'officier fait la même demande a la Fille, qui de son côté fait la même réponse. Alors l'officier prononce à haute voix, 'M.— et N.— la Loi vous unit.' Aprés quoi les Mariés vont à leur propres Eglise s'ils le veulent. L'age de la majorité est fixés a vingt deux ans.

"Dans chaque arrondissement l'enfant qui vient de naître est portè par la sage femme accompagnée du Père et des deux Témoins. On ecrit sur un Registre son nom de Famille et ses présents noms avec le jour auquel il est presenté. Ils ont aussi un Registre pour les Morts.

"Le Gouvernement à present ne reconnait point de Religion particulière mais il donne la liberté à toutes."

What is the effect of this improvement, the fruits of that enlightened philosophy, which has endeavoured to supersede Christianity by reducing the marriage vow from a holy and religious institution, an appointment of God to a mere civil contract which may be divorced at pleasure ? A state of moral depravity has resulted from it,

quiet. The Sermon was upon Job XIX. 29. " Be
ye afraid of the sword : for wrath bringeth the
punishments of the sword, and ye may know there
is a judgment." He treated at length upon the
final judgment, gave the usual arguments in an
impressive manner, and then insisted strongly on
the free will of man which he stated to be consistent with the infinite wisdom and foreappoint-
ment of God though his faculties were not adequate to the explaining how. He concluded with
a most solemn and affecting exhortation. The
latter part of the LVIII Psalm was sung, and the
preacher offered another prayer in which he
petitioned for blessings on the Church of Christ
in general, on such part of it as might still exist in
France and on the congregation present in particular, on the Government established, and
especially on the " Heroes Pacificateurs " etc.
He introduced and pronounced the final bene-
diction in the most impressive manner I ever
heard. " The efficacy of the words I utter depends
upon the Will of that Spirit on whose Authority
I use them, and on the frame of mind in which you
hear them. They can be beneficial only to those
who yield to the influence of that Spirit, and strive
to obey the Laws of Religion." Then after a
solemn pause he delivered the Blessing. His
manner was very earnest, and he used considerable
action but it was of a chaste and dignified kind
which gave additional effect to all he uttered. In

manner and delivery I wish I could preach as
M. Marron does.

The contrast between this service, and that of
the Roman Catholic is very striking. Though
what is going on in the Churches can be considered
but as mere shreds and patches of their worship,
little patterns of the pomp of the Romish ritual,
used by stealth through the connivance of those
in power, for the Government has not yet recognized any religion ; yet it is sufficient to fill a
Protestant with disgust at its idolatry and
absurdity, and to make him very grateful for his
deliverance from it. To see grave old men making
bows to crucifixes, walking about with candles in
their hands, crossing themselves, forming little
processions from one side of the altar to the other,
muttering prayers in an unknown tongue etc.
strikes me as dreadful mockery of that God who
required to be worshipped in spirit and in truth.

Francis dined with Lord Cornwallis.

Bonaparte at the Tuileries

Nov. 30.

Francis, Mr. Webb and myself took a long walk
in the gardens of the Tuileries. One side sheltered
from the wind and opposed to the sun contained
more of the beau monde of Paris than we had yet
seen. But there was hardly a being among them
who bore the appearance of a gentleman. Many
wear beards, or immense whiskers or mustaches.

THE FIRST CONSUL, 1801-2.
FROM AN ENGRAVING PURCHASED IN PARIS BY
REV. DAWSON WARREN

The military especially seem to consider these as indispensable appendages. I should think that nearly a third of the persons we met were military, but a great majority of them were very dirty and untidy.

Bonaparte occupies one part of the Palace, Le Brun the Third Consul the other. Sentinels are posted in great numbers round the building. It is said that Bonaparte passes fourteen hours of every day in business, that his activity is astonishing, and that his eye seems to pervade all the departments of the State. He can therefore spare very little time for amusement or society, but ambition and happiness never went together.

I was told this morning that the First Consul keeps a chère amie[1] in the city whom he privately visits now and then, walking out incognito wrapped up in a great coat. The other day after a nocturnal excursion of this kind, he sent a confidential aide de camp to the Minister of Police with orders to bring all the reports sent in by the spies of the preceding night. The Aide de-Camp was expressly directed to bring them away without allowing the Minister to quit the room or to make the least alteration. Bonaparte found on examining these reports that they contained an exact history of his own wanderings, while he flattered himself he

---

[1] This may possibly refer to Madame Grassini. According to Mr. Tighe Hopkins (*The Women Napoleon Loved*, pp. 173–85), his liaison with Mlle. George [1787–1867] did not begin till the winter of 1802–3, but the recent biographers of this remarkable woman seem to regard the use of dates as superfluous.

F

had been able to elude their vigilance. He returned the papers to the Minister with many commendations of his attention and zeal, but it is supposed was a little vexed withal. Francis knows that one of the livery servants is a spy, and reports the conversation of the dinner table. We are all well aware that we are closely watched.

Lord Cornwallis leaves Paris for Amiens

Lord Cornwallis set off this morning [Nov. 30] for Amiens, and is to sleep at Clermont tonight. He took leave of the Chief Consul yesterday,[1] but went in no great state, considering what means he has brought with him for shew and parade. A coach and pair with three footmen was all. When the Marquis and his party went the other day to see Malmaison, Madame Bonaparte ordered every part of it to be open to them. The salle-à-Manger was the last room shewn, and in it a very elegant collation was set out.

Francis dined with Citoyen Laforest,[2] Secretary

[1] According to Marquis Cornwallis (see *Correspondence*, Vol. III, pp. 399–404), his private farewell audience with the First Consul took place on 28 Nov.

[2] Antoine René Charles Mathurin Laforest [1756–1846]. There was not strictly speaking a Minister of Agriculture in 1801–2. At that time the department of agriculture was administered by the Home Office. Laforest replaced Barbé-Marbois as French Consul at New York in 1788, returning to Paris seven years later. After the *coup d'état* of 18 Brumaire he was placed at the head of the Post Office. In 1800 he discharged the duties of First Secretary of Legation at Lunéville. He was Foreign Minister for a brief period in 1814, after occupying the post of Ambassador at Madrid during five years.

to the Post Office. He gave no very delightful account of the dinner. The lady of the house was ugly and vulgar, and most of the citizens wore beards of a week's growth.

Hill and I went to the Théâtre Français to see Melanie a new Tragedy of La Harpe and a favourite with the Parisian public. It was interesting but very long. A beautiful girl is doomed by a savage father to take the veil. A lover intercedes in vain, then her mother, then a venerable Priest, and lastly the poor damsel herself who begs, kneels, and faints all in vain, till at last she dies in despair. Every body was in tears, and the plaudits were equal to any noise I ever heard. At the conclusion when Melanie was called to come upon the stage they were absolutely riotous. L'école des Maris, a laughable comedy of Molière finished the amusement.

Dec. 1.

A walk with Hill formed the only variety after the French lesson, he studies with me and is a very agreable companion.

Francis took me in the evening to Madame Semonville.[1] Her daughter is the widow of General Joubert. On the day after their marriage he was ordered to join the Army, and was killed a few weeks after at the battle of Novi. The nation

---

[1] See also Berry *Letters and Journal*, Vol. II, p. 144. Mlle. de Montholon was married to General Joubert on 16 July, 1799, when he was ordered to take the command of the army in Italy. He was killed on 15 August following.

sympathised with her. A funeral fête (fête funébre) what odd words to put together! was celebrated in the Champ de Mars, at which Sieyès delivered an oration. His memory was also honoured by a decree, which gave the name of Rue Joubert to the street in which he had resided. Mr. Merry had dined with us, and we went to the Lady's party as soon as he had taken leave. We were a great deal too soon, but I was much amused in chatting with Madame Joubert a very beautiful and agreable woman, while Francis devoted himself to her mother. I was only sensible of making one mistake. I praised the fine countenance of a Sèvres bust which I supposed to be that of the First Consul but she told me with a sigh "C'est le Général Joubert." In half an hour the company began to assemble, and a pretty set they were; the men as dirty; black cropped hair; large whiskers; unshorn chins, many of them in boots. No one would tolerate a footman in the room who was so untidily dressed. This is Republican taste, and they considered it the English fashion. Francis's dress and gentleman-like manners will I think correct these notions. The ladies were a little better in their appearance excepting the prevailing taste for exposure,[1] and

[1] On 3 Jan., 1802, George Jackson writes thus to his mother at Bath :—

"I am afraid to undertake to supply my sister with the information she asks for respecting French fashions. 'What materials are most in vogue?' she enquires; I really do not know. Mr.

MAD.^{ME} BONAPARTE.

JOSEPHINE BONAPARTE IN 1801-2
FROM A CONTEMPORARY ENGRAVING PURCHASED BY THE REV. DAWSON
WARREN DURING HIS STAY IN PARIS

I to mention a few of them it would convey to your mind no idea of their form or beauty. When finished it will be a wonderful collection. They have erected in the garden some of the larger things, such as pillars, aqueducts, mausoleums and small temples. In one part of this garden is a most curious appearance, above 300 statues of the Virgin Mary, our Saviour, kings, prelates, monks, men, women, birds, beasts etc. many of them mutilated, and all strewed promiscuously on the ground. I cannot describe my sensations as I sauntered among them. I fancied myself to be amid the relics of some mighty conflict, that I was walking over the field of battle on which the spirits of infidelity had just routed the demons of superstition.

We dined together at home, and had a pleasant evening. Mr. Webb's fund of anecdotes makes him a very agreeable companion. I am never tired of these domestic parties. They remind me of home, my own dear home. I begin to be sick of Paris.

A Walk with the Minister

Dec. 4th.

A walk with Francis was the chief variety of the morning. A curious and iniquitous law of the Republic was mentioned by him, the law of hostages. Under this, if the purchaser of any national estates or *biens patrimoniaux* should be

injured or plundered, he might come upon the
next person he met who was of the old regime
whether the author of the mischief or no and take
satisfaction ; thus making them as it were hostages
for the safety of true Republicans. Bonaparte has
repealed this law, but there are many still remaining almost as bad, which I suppose he preserves
to keep refractory spirits in order.

Fox and Sheridan at the French Institute

We talked also of the National Institute, an
association of learned men for the purposes of
cultivating and promoting science. Among many
other Englishmen Charles James Fox[1] and Sheridan
were candidates for the honour of admission.
The clearsighted and virtuous Citizens rejected
Charles Fox on account of the immorality of his
private character and elected Sheridan.

The English seen through French Spectacles

We all went to the Théâtre Français this evening, and saw La Coquette Corrigée a good comedy
very well acted, the title of which tells its object.
L'Anglais à Bordeaux was the entertainment, but

---

[1] On 29 July, 1802, Fox set out on a tour through the Nether-
lands, Holland, and France. While at Paris he had several
interviews with Bonaparte, which were mercilessly caricatured
by Gillray and the elder Cruikshank. He paid a short visit to
Lafayette and reached home on 17 Nov. Although he pronounced
the First Consul to be " a young man intoxicated with success,"
he was convinced of his good faith in the matter of the Peace.

somewhat stupid. A party of Englishmen are taken prisoners in a frigate and appear on the stage to talk broken French. The dresses were English, but they have so little idea of our manners that they represented us saluting each other by embracing and kissing both cheeks. A Frenchman told me a story of an actor who came up from Flanders to appear at this theatre. The character he had acquired in the country raised considerable expectations, but when he came out he proved to be a miserable stick. He was experiencing some expressions of disapprobation from the audience when he came to the line, " Dans tel triste embarras quel parti faut-il prendre ? " A wag cried out " Il faut prendre la Poste, et retourner en Flandres."

The British Minister moves to the Hôtel Caraman

Dec. 5.

We enjoyed the comfort of a removal to the Hotel Caraman, Rue Dominique,[1] where Francis has a most elegant and comfortable suite of apartments. The luxury I feel in sitting down to write to you in this clean delightful room is very great. My last habitation was dirty, smoky, and cold.

[1] The Rue Dominique, in the heart of the Faubourg St. Germain, on the southern side of the Seine, runs from the Rue des Saints Pères to the Champ de Mars. Berthier in the Rue de Varennes, Chaptal in the Rue de Grenelle, Fouché in the Quai Malaquai, and Talleyrand in the Rue du Bac, were all near neighbours of the British Minister.

This is in all respects the reverse, yet the rooms
we occupy are large and lofty, with a south aspect
looking into a large garden tastefully laid out.
But I hope to give you a description and perhaps
a sketch of it in the course of a day or two.

M. de las Heras an old Spanish friend of Francis's dined here, a pleasant talkative man whom
perhaps you remember in London. He is not here
in any diplomatic character.

The non arrival of a Messenger keeps us in a
state of suspense about our appearance at the
First Consul's audience tomorrow. Francis more
I am sure from more attention to our gratification
than his own, has sent to ask for places at the
Palace, that we may at all events see the Parade.

Bonaparte as we saw him

Dec. 6.

No Messenger has arrived with Francis's credentials. So the audience was of course given up.
And no answer came to the application which
Francis made for places. Hill and I therefore set
off to try if we could not by bribery or other means
obtain admission to the Tuileries. We found the
Sentinels and gate keepers vigilant and incorrup-
tible and returned to the Hotel. Francis in the
meantime had received a very polite answer from
Talleyrand inclosing a few general tickets and one
to a particular place for himself. He was therefore dressing in his Light Horse Volunteer Regi-

PALAIS DU GOUVERNEMENT.

LAISSEZ ENTRER les deux personnes munies du présent Billet, pour la Parade du *Quinze Frimaire* an 10 de la République française.

Le Général Gouverneur du Palais,

Duroc

Liberté.   *Egalité.*

Paris, le ·· *an* · *de la République française, une et indivisible.*

Le Secrétaire d'Etat

ORDER OF ADMISSION TO THE REVIEW OF 6 DEC. 1801, GRANTED TO REV. DAWSON WARREN AND SIGNED BY DUROC

mentals to go there. Hill and I walked back to
the Palace and got places on the staircase. It was
lined on each side by grenadiers behind whom we
stood. After a little while the drums beat, the
grenadiers presented arms, the folding doors at
the head of the stairs were thrown open, and the
hero appeared. He was preceded by four Aids-de-
Camps with their hats on. He himself and the
General Officers who followed him were uncovered.
I shall probably never again have so good a view
of him. I saw him as he was descending the upper
part of the staircase and he passed close to me.
Of course you expect me to describe him ; but I
was disappointed. There is nothing remarkable
to describe. The great soul of the Héros Pacificateur, the Conqueror of Italy, and the terror of
great part of Europe is lodged in a small light body
about five feet four inches high which was covered
by an ill-made crimson velvet coat with gold lace
and embroidery on the collar and sleeves ; white
pantaloons and boots. This with a plain cocked
hat and National cockade completed the Consular Dress.[1] His countenance appeared to be

[1] Mr. Warren adds the following description of the First
Consul from another pen :—

" Bonaparte was clothed in the Consular dress, scarlet velvet,
slightly embroidered : he passed through the line which was
formed for him with rather a quick, unstately step, and evidently
courted not attention : if you ask of me a description of his
person, which I had twice an excellent opportunity of observing,
being each time in front of the row through which he passed and
repassed, I shall refer you to the busts which this nation of

thin, sallow and unhealthy. The lightening of his eye which is so often talked of was not then flashing nor was there any thing in his appearance which would have led me to suppose that he was any thing more than an attorney's clerk. He walked hastily and without looking around him. There were no shouts of enthusiasm. He passed by as a shadow and made no impression upon me. I endeavoured to follow him out of the grand door but was stopt by the guards. I then climbed into a window of the hall and saw him ride along the line. He was mounted on a fine white charger, which a French gentleman standing by told me was 22 years old, and was a great favourite of the late King Louis XVI who used to ride him at reviews and on other public occasions. Bonaparte appeared to more advantage on horseback. I observed that he rode with very long stirrups as if the soles of his feet scarcely touched them, he was attended by several General Officers who were

iconolaters have doubtless exported into England. Bonaparte is a small but well-proportioned man : his most pale, sallow, and emaciated countenance bears indubitable marks of deep and fearful thinking : a dejection and melancholy which is communicative have possessed it, and are only relieved by his dark and piercing eye, which, though it wanders not with vagrant curiosity and idle sportfulness, by no means partakes of the general unhealthiness of his appearance. His hair is dark, and somewhat long, uncurled, unpowdered. The care-worn countenance of Bonaparte impresses one with the idea that it has never known the sweet relaxation of a smile : of late probably it has not ; he is said to keep his left hand in ignorance of what his right hand does, and to have no bosom friend, but, like Junius, to be the sole repository of his own secrets."

THE FIRST CONSUL IN GALA UNIFORM, 1801-2
FROM A CONTEMPORARY COLOUR-PRINT

also well-mounted. After riding along the line, a circle was formed and he delivered some sabres and muskets as honorary rewards. I was not near enough to hear his words if he spoke anything, but the whole seemed dull and flat. The by-stander said he was out of spirits. In marching the veterans went first. I asked many questions about the regiments present, but unfortunately cannot recollect the answers. If I could they would not probably interest you. The Grenadiers were fine men, and some of Cavalry had fine horses. The Consular Guards are indulged with higher pay and greater privileges.

Francis's regimentals attracted particular attention. They are very handsome but it is the dress of a private. When the nature of the service undertaken by the Light Horse Volunteers was explained, and it was mentioned that the Duke of Dorset[1] was Francis's right hand man in the ranks it occasioned many expressions of surprise and some of admiration. An Officer's sash, which was offered him by the Corps before he left England, would have added nothing to his real dignity, but it would have deprived him of an opportunity of shewing Frenchmen what English patriotism is, and how the subjects of George III serve their King and Country.

[1] John Frederick Sackville, Duke of Dorset [1745–1799]. He was educated at Westminster and a trustee of the school. His successor George John Frederick was only eight years old in 1801.

Mr. Ogilvy a Scotchman called on Francis after the review in his Highland dress. A fine stout man whose costume and person excited also much notice at the Tuileries. Hill and he recognised each other as old friends. Francis asked him to dinner during which I found he had been some years ago very intimate with my brother. He sets out this evening for London, but I shall not trouble him with a packet. I like the Government messengers.

The Hotel Caraman Described

Dec. 7.

If I had not the pleasure of writing to you my dear Wife this full account of all I see and hear I feel, I should be heartily sick of my sojourn here. But this fills up the remnants of time in a manner most interesting to me and you give me the greatest encouragement by expressing yourself gratified with my packets. I will now give you some particulars of our house, establishment and the manner of living, for I am sure you are curious to know them.

First for the Mansion I send you a little drawing of it ; and a rough sketch of a plan.[1]

---

[1] This plan is now reproduced. On 3 August, 1805, Theresa Tallien (formerly Cabarrus) became the wife of Comte François Joseph Philippe Caraman, whom she had met at the house of Madame de Staël, and who shortly afterwards succeeded to all the family honours and wealth. See *Madame Tallien*, by L. Gastine. John Lane, London, 1913.

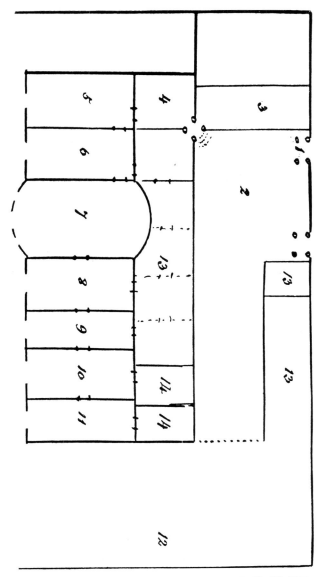

GROUND-PLAN OF THE APARTMENTS OCCUPIED BY THE
BRITISH MISSION IN THE HÔTEL CARAMAN, RUE ST
DOMINIQUE, PARIS, DEC. 1801–APRIL 1802

1. Entrance from the Rue Dominique.
2. Court Yard.
3. Servant's Hall.
4. Entrance Hall.
5. Mr. Webb's Room.
6. Dining Room, large and handsome.
7. A very elegant drawing room richly gilt and ornamented, blue damask furniture.
8. Francis's Study and bedroom fitted up in a similar style.
9. Francis's dressing room fitted up with prints.
10. My room with a closet.
11. Hunter's room.
12. Coach Houses and stables over which Hill's room is.
13. Offices for the domestics etc.
14. Apartments occupied by the old master of the hotel, the venerable Marquis de Caraman, and his servants.

All the furniture is rich and splendid.

The Story of the Caramans

Having mentioned this nobleman and his faithful domestic I must say a little more of them. Before the Revolution the Marquis was one of the richest men in France. He was proprietor of the principal part of the Canal in Languedoc, for his share of which the old Government offered his father above £600,000 sterling, and he had very large estates. This hotel was his town residence

G

and he occupied it with a large family and sixty servants. When the Revolution broke out he found it necessary to quit the country. Before he went his Maître d'hotel assisted him in burying the family plate and jewels in the garden. As soon as he was safe this servant denounced him and appeared to be a fierce Republican by which he contrived to keep possession of the hotel. A little while since M. Caraman got his name erased from the List of Emigrants and returned to Paris. His faithful domestic received him with joy, restored him all he had saved, and now waits upon his Master who is between 70 and 80 years old with the most respectful attention. This Hotel and the plate form the wreck of the Marquis's immense property.[1]

Mr. Jackson's Establishment

So much for the house now for the establishment. Hunter, Butler and valet, Stephen underbutler. A coachman etc. Two footmen, man-cook etc. The two first are the only English servants, and they are two excellent ones. Francis gives the white family liveries, and you know him well enough to be satisfied that every domestic arrangement is perfect in its kind. The whole is a piece of clock work. I was with Francis when the hatter brought home the servants dress hats. Hunter

[1] The Caramans subsequently inherited the possessions of the Savoy branch of the family.

A PARISIAN TEA-PARTY IN 1801

FROM "LE THÉ PARISIEN SUPRÊME BON TON AU COMMENCEMENT DU 19ᵐᵉ SIÈCLE."—THE RARE AQUATINT

ADRIEN GODFREY AFTER F. J. HARRIET

shewed one of them to his master with a tricolored cockade in it. The hatter was ordered in and directed to take out the cockades. He said they were used by command of the First Consul which every body complied with. Francis replied " I receive no orders from any one except my own Master, His Britannic Majesty. You will either take out those cockades or take away those hats." The astonished hatter complied immediately with the former of these alternatives.

Our manner of living is breakfast at nine. Dinner at 5. When alone three dishes and soup removed for a Rôti. A second course of three, chiefly sweets; and a dessert of three. Claret, Burgundy and champagne. Coffee. Sometimes tea two or three hours afterwards, if any one asks for it.[1] I have been endeavouring to remember a bill-of-fare, but the names of the dishes perplex me, and the variety seems endless.

[A month later George Jackson wrote to his mother : " As you ask for domestic news, you may perhaps care to hear that my brother having made up his accounts to the end of the year, finds that, limiting himself to the very moderate style of living he has adopted here, £4000 would barely bring him round the year. He has but one carriage and one pair of horses, no extra groom, and no

---

[1] The English fondness for tea was now emulated in Paris. The reproduction of Harriet's drawing gives an excellent idea of a French tea-party in 1801.

saddle horses, but those that are hired. This calculation proves, that the expense of living in Paris
is increased by at least one-third since the revolution.'']

A Sad Accident

A melancholy story has just attracted our
attention. Mrs. Clark lost her husband at the
Hotel d'Angleterre. He was a young man going
with her to visit the south of France. They had
hastened to Paris to see the Great Fête,[1] and were
in the Booth which gave way with a great croud
upon it. She was not much hurt, but his back
was broken, and from the moment of the accident
has not been able to move a limb. Francis wrote
to her to offer any services in his power, and had
a verbal acknowledgment. Her servant described
the poor widow to be in the most afflicting state
but she had given orders for embalming the body
with the view of conveying it to England. Bonaparte sent his own surgeon and made enquiries
immediately after the accident.

I send you two prints of the First Consul, and
his wife which are said to be very like. I can
answer for his being a strong resemblance. I
would enclose a medallion could it be conveyed
by a letter.

[1] That in honour of the Peace given on 9 Nov. (18 Brumaire)
by order of the First Consul.

A PARIS PROMENADE IN 1801–2

FROM THE COLOURED AQUATINT OF L. P. DEBUCOURT

The Paris Print Shops

Dec. 8.

After dispatching a messenger, an errand which
always keeps the house in a bustle for some hours,
I took a walk by myself, sauntering through the
streets without any specific object. I cast my
eyes as I passed upon a few of the printshops.
The depravity of this place is most awful. In
London few good artists will misemploy their
talents upon indecent subjects, in Paris they seem
to work on little else ; and every seller of prints
hangs round his shop articles that would not be
tolerated for a moment among us. Books of a
similar tendency stare you in the face at every
stall, and are offered to you at every corner. I
never walk out but I am accosted by people with
an offer to introduce me to their beautiful cousin
or friend ; and females in the most extraordinary
light dresses parade the most public walks and
accost passers by at all hours of the day. Corruption of morals reigns here with unlimited sway,
and cankers the very heart of all Society.

An Evening's Amusements

At six Francis took me to dine with Ehrensward
the Swedish Minister. A party of 14 men. Tolerably pleasant. Abundance of good eating and
drinking. Too much of it indeed for my taste.
I think I have eaten of twenty things, yet I

refused four out of five which the officious servants put before me. I am sick of fine dinners and shall return to my steak at home with peculiar feelings of satisfaction in what is comfortable. All people seem to be very fond of the English, and if they can talk three words of our language they use the acquisition sometimes to my annoyance for it is more difficult to understand them. I imagine my broken French to be occasionally as annoying to my new friends, but they are always good humoured and help me out, sometimes to meanings I never intended.

After dinner we went to the Opera at the Théâtre de la Republique where the musick, singing, scenery and machinery are considered very superior.[1] I thought the ladies squalled too much. The house is very handsome, but I should find fault with the heavy pillars if it were not for a curious contrivance ; they are hollow and contain little boxes for two or three persons. Madame Bonaparte's box is hung with crimson velvet and gold lace where she sits in state. The first Consul occupies a close private box beneath hers.[2] I sat next a very pleasant Frenchman to whom I was introduced at Baron Ehrensward's, and who answered many of my enquiries about

[1] There is an admirable illustration of this theatre at the corner of the Rue Louvois and the Rue de Richelieu by Blanchard Père after Courvoisier. It was formerly known as the Théâtre des Arts and the Académie Royal de Musique.

[2] George Jackson calls it a *loge grillée.*

Madame Bonaparte. He represented her manners
to be most elegant and pleasing, full of affability
and attention. She begins to assume a great deal
more state than is consistent with the theory of
Republican equality. She has a very large train
of servants ; a little while ago they were dressed
in a uniform very like a livery ; and now they are
never to speak to her. An officer of the Consular
Guard is always in waiting to receive and deliver
her commands, announce her carriage etc. She
gives very large parties on the seventh of every
Decade, to which those only are invited who have
been introduced to the First Consul. The establishment may be judged of from their frequently
giving dinners at the Tuileries of 180 covers.

Hill joined us at the Opera, and we went with
Francis where we were to meet the first company
in Paris assembled at a ball. The entertainment
was given in three rooms not sufficient for so large
a party. Either the men improve in their dress
or it was a different set, for about a fourth of them
looked like gentlemen half of whom carried cocked
hats. If you ask me what was the proportion of
pretty women, I should say that one in ten might
pass tolerably, and one in twenty might be
accounted handsome. The universal exposure of
the bust must proceed I suppose from an enthu-
siastic admiration of the antique which they have
acquired from the statues in the Museum. I trust
our Countrywomen will teach them better fashions.

We met there Lucien Bonaparte who is just
returned from Spain. The First Consul's sister-
in-law was also there with a very light complexion
and two or three more of the family whom I shall
be better able to describe when I shall see them
again.

English Visitors

Dec. 9.

This morning was rendered delightful by the
arrival of a courier. The rain prevented even a
walk. Mr. Blaquiere son of an Irish Peer[1] dined
here.

After dinner two English officers sent in their
names with a request to be admitted. On being
admitted they expressed their surprise at not
seeing their friend Mr. Thomas Jackson whom they
thought to be the Minister. But they sat down
and gave us some very interesting anecdotes of
the Expedition to Egypt. They were just returned
from that country. They told us 26,000 Frenchmen had recently embarked from thence for
France. What an honour for English Troops to
have driven them out of Egypt with a very
inferior force. They represented the French as
having been so detested in that Country that not
one of them could venture out of the camp
without the greatest hazard of being murdered,

---

[1] John Blaquiere [1732–1812]. Son of a French emigrant.
Served under Lord Harcourt as Secretary of Legation in France,
1771–2 ; Chief Secretary in Ireland, 1772–7 ; Privy Councillor,
1774, and a Baronet, 1784. Raised to an Irish peerage in 1800.

while an Englishman could travel in any part of Egypt with perfect safety. The inhabitants carried their dislike to the French so far they killed and threw into the Nile such of their women as visited the camp. They had some reason for this aversion. I am sorry for the credit of our common nature to tell you such a story as I am now going to relate upon the authority of these gentlemen. Admirers of Bonaparte! What will you say?

Ill-natured gossip about Bonaparte

When General Bonaparte had taken Jaffa[1] upwards 2300 Turks surrendered themselves prisoners on the faith of his promises. He sent for his Commissary and found that he could not conveniently spare so much of his provisions as such a number would require. He reflected also that it might be injurious to his interests to set them at liberty. So three days after the engagement he ordered three battalions of his Army to conduct them to a retired place two miles off, and massacre them. The order was punctually obeyed. They were fired upon till they all fell, and the wounded were dispatched with sabres. What a foul blot in a man's character is this! I will tell you of a worse.

[1] For the correct version of this story see Dr. J. Holland Rose's *Life of Napoleon*, Vol. I, pp. 201, 203–4, and 211–13.

Stories of Sir Sidney Smith and Sir Ralph
Abercromby

You remember how gallantly Sir Sidney Smith defended Acre, when with an inferior force and comparatively small resources he checked the conqueror in his career, and saved the Ottoman Empire from imminent destruction. Bonaparte on this repulse was distressed to know how he ould dispose of 300 of his wounded men. His proud spirit could not stoop to ask a favour of his brave adversary, and he knew that leaving them to the Turks was exposing them to a certain and miserable death. He therefore caused a large quantity of poisoned bread to be made. The poor fellows eat it and died. The Army pursued its march free from the encumbrance of them. These things are not known in France. The Army now on its return will quickly circulate them. The man who mixed the poison in the bread is now suffering under the stings of conscience, he has written an account of the expedition to Egypt, and one of the Officers, Sir Robert Wilson[1] says it is now in the Press. Surely it must have some effect upon the People of France.[2]

These gentlemen spoke in the highest terms of

[1] General Sir Robert Thomas Wilson [1777–1849]. Educated at Westminster School. Was knighted in 1801. Like Admiral Sir Sidney Smith, he was well known in Paris through the greater part of his somewhat adventurous career.

[2] See also Dr. J. Holland Rose's *Life of Napoleon*, Vol. I, pp. 201, 204–20, and 413.

Sir Ralph Abercromby, and Sir Sidney Smith ; and mentioned this anecdote. During the engagement in which the first of these heroes lost his life, he was standing after being wounded talking with Sir Sidney, who complained he had just lost both his horse and his sword. A French dragoon rode up and attempted to cut down Sir Ralph but the General with an activity and strength wonderful in a man of his age, evaded the blow, seized the hilt of the sword and wrenched it from the man's hand. He immediately presented it to Sir Sidney expressing himself happy in being able to supply a part of his wants. The dragoon rode off, but a few of the 42nd Regt. came up and fired at and killed him. In two minutes after another officer rode up to whom Sir Sidney applied for the loan of the horse his orderly dragoon was riding. Before the dragoon could dismount a ball took his head off. " Surely," said Sir Sidney, " this is something like Destiny."

In France Sir Sidney Smith is much admired and often talked of.[1] How the First Consul would like to see him may be doubted for he has never yet been successfully opposed except by this gallant countryman of ours.

Sir Robert mentioned an extraordinary Regiment raised by Bonaparte in Egypt of 400 men

[1] Admiral Sir William Sidney Smith [1764–1840]. Sir Sidney Smith died at Paris and is buried in the Père Lachaise cemetery. During his lengthy residence in the French capital he was intimately associated with several Masonic Lodges.

who were superbly dressed and mounted on Dromedaries, animals capable of carrying great weights, and of living a long time without water. They were sent to places where horses could not travel to attack caravans and bring home plunder.

As soon as Bonaparte knew how his affairs were going in Egypt, and he seems to have had intelligence wonderfully quick, he agreed on the preliminaries of Peace with England, and did the same thing with a man accredited from the Ottoman Porte. In both these Treaties, the surrender of Egypt, already wrested from him was made an article and received an equivalent.

An Interview with Latude, the Hero of the Bastille

Dec. 10.

During my French lesson yesterday the conversational part of it turned upon the Bastille. M. Le Gros told me that his wife had been instrumental in procuring the liberty of Latude who had been a prisoner 35 years. Seeing how much I was interested in the accounts he gave of that extraordinary man, he offered to introduce me to him. Hill and I went accordingly to call upon him this morning, accompanied by our French Master. Henri Masers de Latude is 78 years old, but strong, active and hearty as a man of half that age. He received us with great civility, and gave us a long account of all implements etc by which he made

Flute

Flagiolet .

Knife

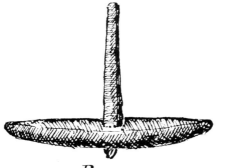

Hammer

Borer.

INSTRUMENTS USED BY LATUDE IN HIS ESCAPE FROM THE BASTILLE,
AFTER SKETCHES MADE FROM THE ORIGINALS BY THE REV. DAWSON WARREN

his escape from the Bastille, and by which he
contrived to sooth the horrors of imprisonment.
He was the only individual who ever escaped from
the Bastille.

On a table, which I suppose was arranged in
expectation of our visit, was placed the right hand
broken from the Bronze statue of Louis XV. That
statue stood in the large square then called the
Place de Louis XV, afterwards " Place de la
Revolution," and now " Place de la Concorde."
" There," said the old man pointing to it, " That
is the hand that gave me such a dreadful blow.
The People when they pulled down the statue
broke it off, and gave it to me. This," he continued, taking up a little musical instrument of
the shape and size of a large fife, " this was my
flute. I made it from a pewter plate. I played
upon it many a long hour in the Bastille. This
was my flageolet." It was of wood and very neat,
" I will give you an air upon it." And he played a
wild sort of whistling ; a succession of notes of
which I could not comprehend the intervals, nor
make out the air ; though he seemed to think it
most excellent music and went on longer than was
necessary to gratify me. " These are my play-
things with which I used to cheat the dull hours.
of captivity, now you must see my working
tools.

" This is the knife with which all the wood work
was carved. I contrived to get a flint and steel,

and shaped this blade from the steel by one of the stones I had pulled out of the wall.

" This hammer was a bolt which after immense labour I got out of the iron grating of my window.

" This is my borer ; you see it is another bolt fixed likewise in a wooden handle. With this I worked my way in one night through a four foot wall into a chimney up which I had to climb that I might get to the top of the tower. To enable me to climb it I made this ladder of wood. You observe how these joints fit one another, when put together they are fastened at each point by two strong pins. These projecting were to support my hands and feet as I climbed.

" This was my saw. I made it from an old iron candlestick. It is rather clumsy but you must remember what materials I had. I cut out the teeth of it with this punch manufactured out of a small bolt.

" Now I must shew you my rope ladder," and he took up a large bundle from the corner of the room. " I made this out of the wood brought me to burn. I covered every round with pieces of my blankets or my clothing as I could spare them that they might not rattle and twisted the ropes out of my linen and silk stockings ; with this having fastened one end of it to a cannon, I descended from a perpendicular height of 180 feet. Fearing that I might be giddy at such a height I made another rope of the same length, and at the time

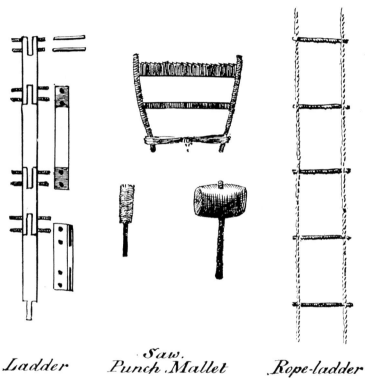

Ladder   *Saw.*
Punch Mallet   *Rope-ladder*

LADDER AND OTHER INSTRUMENTS USED BY LATUDE IN
ESCAPING FROM THE BASTILLE

FROM SKETCHES MADE IN PARIS BY REV. DAWSON WARREN

of my escape fastened one end to the cannon and the other round my body so as to catch me if I lost my hold."

I carefully examined these works or could scarcely have believed the fabrication of them possible. They had occupied him a long course of years, and had always kept alive his hope of deliverance. At the time of his escape he of course left them behind him, and they were preserved in the Bastille as a great curiosity. On the destruction of that prison they were found by the people and given to him.

The Bastille which stood for four centuries the terror of France and the wonder of Europe was destroyed in four hours by a Paris Mob. The building of it was begun in 1370 by Charles V. He erected a tower on each side of the high road and connected them by an arch, as an ornament and defence to the city. Charles VI built four additional towers, calling one of them the Tower of Liberty : united them by a wall six feet thick : and turned the road. It was afterwards fortified by a wide and deep ditch.

The Armoury used to contain 40,000 muskets, but it was removed several years since to the Hôtel des Invalides.

The establishment of the Bastille consisted of

A Governor
who had a good house within the walls
Lieutenant   A Commissary

A Major and 2 Adjutants	A Surgeon
100 Invalides	Three Chaplains
An Engineer	Two Confessors
An Entrepreneur des Bâtimens	Two keepers of archives

The strictest discipline was enforced and the slightest deviation from it severely punished.

The great object of this prison was the detention of state delinquents, but it became too frequently an instrument of private malice and intrigue, and under the direction of Roman Catholic bigotry an engine of persecution. A Register of the Prisoners containing the dates and causes of commitment has been printed from the documents found after its demolition. It shews that the number of those unfortunate victims has been greatly exaggerated, but it shews also that they were often confined on the most frivolous pretences. When the Mob entered the Bastille there were only seven prisoners found within its walls. I extract a few years of the highest and lowest numbers.

In 1663 there were 54 prisoners
,, 1664 ,, ,, 13 ,,
,, 1686 ,, ,, 147 ,, mostly on the score of religion
,, 1695 ,, ,, 7 ,,
,, 1733 ,, ,, 63 ,,
,, 1759 ,, ,, 37 ,,
,, 1761 ,, ,, 4 ,,

Some were confined on charges of the most atrocious treason, some on the slightest suspicion, some for heresy, or disobedience to a Royal

Mandate. Several owed their confinement to the publication of libels or indecent books, satirical verses or epigrams. In two or three instances sons procured the imprisonment of their fathers and wives that of their husbands because they were dissipating their property. The following entry is translated literally.

" 1733. Malbay, who assisted the Duke of Nivernois to ruin himself. He was committed to the Bastille at the instance of the Duke de Nevers. This prisoner had a very beautiful wife."

At the beginning of the Revolution this fortress was under the command of M. de Launay. Some days before the Populace attacked it he prepared for its defence placed 15 cannon in advantageous situations and delivered ammunition to the men. The garrison was then 32 Swiss Guards and 82 Invalides. On the 13th of July the Governor drew his men into the interior of the castle and placed 12 Centinels on the Towers. These Sentinels were now and then fired at.

Next morning three persons stating themselves to be Deputies of the City presented themselves at the gate, and demanded an interview with the Governor. De Launay refused to admit the crowd which followed them, but sent four of his officers as hostages for their safety. The object of these Deputies was to persuade the Governor to give up the place, and if they failed in that to seduce the military ; The soldiers promised they would

H

not fire unless they were absolutely attacked. The Deputies promised that all should be quiet and retired. In half an hour the Mob assembled in large parties armed with muskets, sabres, axes or any thing they could procure, crying " Down with the Bastille." They called on the soldiers to quit the towers. The replies and entreaties of the garrison were of no avail. The Populace pressed forward, and two men had the audacity to climb up and break with their hatchets the chains which suspended the drawbridge. Emboldened by this success the crowd rushed in, and ran to the second bridge firing musquets at the men stationed on the towers. Thus provoked the garrison fired a few shot and the mob fled in the utmost disorder. After a little time the Deputies appeared again but were fearful of entering and retired. The mob attacked the second bridge, the governor ordered the men to fire, by which several were killed and the rest retreated, but continued to fire on the officers and men who appeared upon the towers.

The rioters then brought three loads of straw and set fire to it but without effect. The Mob was then reinforced by the Gardes Françaises who brought two four-pounders to bear upon the bridge, but all was fruitless the place was much too strong for such assailants, had the garrison been faithful and resolute.

Fear within did more than force without. The subaltern officers entreated the Governor to surrender. His indecision increased the alarm and danger. He took up a match with an intention of blowing up the magazine, but was stopt by two men who suspected his intention. He addressed the garrison declaring that he had much rather leap from the battlements than be massacred by the people, whose fury there was no way of escaping. The soldiers replied that it was impossible to fight much longer, and they had rather resign themselves to anything than slaughter more of their fellow-citizens. They proposed hoisting a white flag, and offering to capitulate. As they had no such flag the Governor gave them his handkerchief. It was displayed upon a stick and paraded three times round the platform accompanied by a drum. The mob paid no attention and continued firing till all shew of defense had ceased. They then approached nearer calling out " Lower the bridge." A Swiss officer made himself heard and proposed that the garrison should be allowed to march out with the honours of war. This was answered by a great cry of " No." He then wrote a form of capitulation, proposing that they should lay down their arms and deliver up the place on receiving a solemn promise of personal safety. The reply was " Lower the bridge and you shall not be hurt." On this assurance the Governor gave up the keys, the gate was opened and the bridge lowered.

The most horrible confusion ensued. Crowds

poured in. They seized the invalides who had deposited their arms against the wall. The Swiss were dressed in linen frocks and were mistaken for prisoners. They broke open the apartments of the officers, threw out the furniture and committed every devastation in their power. Other parties rushed in and fired upon them by mistake and many fell victims of their mutual blindness and fury.

At length the Invalides who were not massacred on the spot were conducted like slaves to the Hotel de Ville, and were exposed as they went to every insult and torment. The sight of two of their comrades hanging before the door was a fresh aggravation of their misery. An officer of the City came out and said "You have fired upon your fellow citizens, and you shall be hanged." A thousand voices exclaimed "Give them up to us, we will hang them." The soldiers of the Gardes-Françaises interfered, rescued 22 of them, and escorted them to a place of safety.

The Governor was seized by some ferocious wretches who hurried him to the Place de Grève, severed his head from his body, and carried it on a pike through the streets.

The Bastille contained only seven prisoners when it was thus destroyed. The revolutionary despots who usurped the powers of Government overcrowded the prisons with thousands who had scarcely incurred a suspicion, and after a shadow of trial often without even that led them out to be slaughtered in order to make room for fresh victims. Such are the fruits of Mob-Power—such the effects of violent Revolutions—such the consequences of overturning established Governments.

Latude occupies apartments in the Hotel or rather Palais de Salms, a magnificent Mansion, the late owner of which the Prince de Salms was driven out by the Revolution. It was bought by a hairdresser for a small sum, and is now let out at low rents to various poor Families. What a strange thing it is to see these elegant apartments richly painted and gilded in the occupation of such tenants. The building is of course hastening to decay, and exhibits a melancholy instance of overthrown grandeur.

M. Le Gros has lent me a *Life of Latude* written by himself and printed eight years ago, which is now very scarce.

H. M. Latude was born in 1723 at the Château of his Father the Marquis de Latude in Languedoc. He was educated for the Army. The peace of 1748 stopped his promotion and he came to Paris. Full of ambition and high spirit he sought for distinction and promotion by the following wild scheme.

Madame de Pompadour was the reigning favorite, and so governed Louis XV and his court that a word of hers could make or ruin the fortune of any man. But she was proud and cruel, and consequently detested. Latude thought he might avail himself of this public indignation which was well known to her, pretend a plot against her life, and secure her favour by discovering it. He sent her by the Post a small box of powder perfectly harmless. He waited on the lady, informed her that such a thing was coming to her, and made up a very alarming story of a conspiracy to poison her. The Marquise expressed the most lively gratitude, and offered him a purse of gold. This he declined but dropped a hint that he was not provided for, and intimated as he thought in the most delicate manner that her patronage was the object of his ambition. She suspected him and desired him to write his name and address. This when compared with the direction of the packet, betrayed him. The next day all his dreams of approaching greatness were destroyed by the arrival of a guard to convey him to the Bastille. He was there stripped of all he had, dressed in coarse clothing which had served several of his predecessors, and shut up in a cell to ruminate upon his folly.

The following day the Lieutenant of the Police came in to examine him. Latude confessed his fault so ingeniously that he gained the good opinion of this officer who promised to intercede for him with Madame Pompadour to procure his pardon. This application was unsuccessful, but procured him the use of some books, the privilege of exercise in the air, and the society of another prisoner, a Jew.

These comforts probably reached the ear and offended the inexorable soul of Mad. Pompadour. In four months time he was removed to the Prison of Vincennes. The discipline there was very strict. A guard was constantly with him to report every word and action. The wretchedness of his mind brought on illness, under which his best remedy was meditating on the means of escape. In about 14 months he effected it in the following manner. He had liberty to walk in the garden two hours every day, accompanied by two turnkeys. The elder of these usually waited for him at the foot of the stairs while the younger came alone to open his room door. At such times he would hasten down to rejoin the other, and the younger turnkey accustomed to find him always safe below never hastened his pace to follow him. One day the moment the door was opened, he glided down the staircase, fastened a door at the foot which shut in the old turnkey, proceeded to an outward door, where he enquired if the confessor was arrived, he was wanted instantly. Latude deceived a second, third and fourth sentinel in the same manner, and in few moments found himself free.

He found means of getting into Paris but the dread of being retaken induced him to throw himself on the mercy of Madame Pompadour.

He drew up a memorial, craved forgiveness and pointed out the place of his retreat. He was immediately arrested and sent again to the Bastille.

His confinement was now more severe than ever. He was thrown into a dungeon with very little light. But his kind friend the Lieutenant in time relieved him by ordering him good diet and the use of books, paper and ink. Latude had the folly to write some satirical lines upon his powerful enemy, they were carried to her, her enmity became inveterate. In answer to an application in his favour she shewed these verses. " See the wretch you plead for, and never mention him to me more." He remained eighteen months when the Lieutenant procured his removal into better quarters and the accommodation of a servant. A man was induced by high wages to leave his wife and family and enter the Bastille. But having done this the regulations of the place forbade his ever going out or holding any correspondence without the walls unless his Master should obtain his liberty. The poor fellow who thus engaged himself in the service of Latude could not long support his situation. He pined and died. This severe affliction was alleviated by the kindness of that friend to whom he had been so much indebted, and D'Alègre another prisoner was put into his room. D'Alègre had also offended Madame Pompadour by writing to her a letter of advice and had equally with Latude experienced the kindness and compassionate Lieutenant, who had always done his utmost to procure their release. He one day put an end to all hope by saying that Madame Pompadour had sworn that her hatred should be eternal, and commanded him never again to mention their names. D'Alègre gave himself up to despair; Latude formed a design for escaping. Probably no prisoner had ever thought there was a possibility of doing so, certainly none had ever been able to effect it. Escape was always considered an absolute impossibility. To any one but Latude it would indeed have appeared impossible to mount a chimney full of grates and bars of iron, to descend from a tower near 200 feet high, to pass a fosse full of water guarded by a high wall, and to escape the numerous centinels posted in all directions. Yet this was accomplished by Latude and his companion in the following manner.

They discovered a space between the floor of their apartment and the ceiling of that below them, and made it the depot for their tools and materials. Of those I have already given you an account. The preparing them occupied about two years. During this time they got out the iron bars and gratings of the chimney. They could only work in the night. On the 25th of February 1756 Latude climbed the chimney the labour of which made his hands and knees raw and gave him great pain.

He drew up the various articles necessary for their escape by a cord, and assisted the ascent of his companion. They were then on the platform of the Bastille and fixed on the Tower de Trésor as most suitable for their purpose. They fastened one end of the ladder to a cannon, and Latude having fixed the spare cord round his body descended. This was very difficult the Battlements overhung the wall he swung in the air and fell back so that it was exceedingly difficult to keep his hold. When safe in the fosse D'Alègre lowered what was necessary and then followed.

The night was dark but it did not rain. They heard a centinel walking a few paces from them. They were therefore compelled to abandon their design of mounting the parapet and crossing the Governor's garden. They went to the right to the wall which separated the fosse of the Bastille from that of the Gate St. Antoine, and began to work with the iron bars. It was the duty of the Ronde-Major to visit sentinels every half hour to ascertain their being awake, Latude and his companion were consequently often disturbed in their work, and slunk down in the water. They were once much terrified by seeing a centinel stop and look over the parapet just above them, but he did not speak and retired. At length after nine hours excessive labour and continued terror they worked a hole through the wall, which was above four feet thick, and found themselves in the Fosse St.

Antoine. As they proceeded towards the high road one of them fell into the Aqueduct and narrowly escaped being drowned. They could hardly crawl from excessive fatigue and cold, yet intense excitement and fear urged them forward till as the City clocks struck 5 they were safe and at liberty.

They met with a Hackney coach and went to the house of M. Silhouette's an old friend of Latude's. He was from home, but they found concealment and every kindness from a relation named Dejean.

The mortification of such an escape stimulated the Police to every exertion in order to retake them. They remained closely concealed under the care of their kind friends for a month, and then quitted Paris separately and in disguise, having agreed to meet at Brussels.

On Latude's arrival there he enquired for his friend D'Alègre. The answers alarmed him, he ordered his supper and slipped out of the house. He got into a passage-boat going to Anvers. In this boat he heard the history of D'Alègre who had been taken up at Brussels. He immediately quitted the boat and walked till he reached Bergen-op-Zoom. There he travelled to Amsterdam, where he arrived in a starving condition for his money had failed him. He subsisted some time on the charity of strangers, till he discovered a relation of his family. He then thought himself safe and happy.

This dream was short. The French Ambassador heard of him, and applied for leave to arrest him. Poor Latude was seized, loaded with irons, treated with every possible insult and cruelty and carried back to Paris. The gaolers of the Bastille received him with fiendish exultation ; they had been punished for his escape, and to prevent the possibility of his doing so again, he was ironed hand and foot and placed in a dungeon.

In this horrible situation he found amusement in training some of the rats which infested his miserable abode, and thus drew consolation from what was at first a torment. They became very sociable with him. He attempted also to train some spiders in the same manner but without success.

It occurred to Latude that he might interest the King in his favour if he could lay before him a plan for increasing the efficiency of an army in the field by arming the serjeants and non-commissioned officers. But paper was refused him. He formed tablets of crumb of bread, took a fish bone for his pen, and drew blood from his arm for ink. The confessor who visited him occasionally promised to transcribe it on paper and present it to the Minister. This excited some interest and procured him the free use of writing materials. He prepared a memorial which was presented to the King. The proposed improvement was adopted, but it brought no liberty to the suggestor.

After waiting three months, he drew up a plan which had occurred to him of forming an establishment for the widows and orphans of soldiers. The expense to be defrayed by a particular tax. The tax was immediately laid, but the charitable part of the scheme forgotten.

Thus Latude languished in Prison. Denied air and exercise his health began to fail, and his strength and spirits sunk under the cruelties he experienced. In moments of despair he made two or three attempts to destroy himself. The surgeon reported his miserable state without effect, till the Seine overflowed its banks and filled the dungeons of the prison. He was then removed to an upper apartment where he had purer air. A pigeon flew into this room and became a great relief to him. The Gaoler demanded remuneration for permission to keep it, and so raised his demands that Latude killed it himself. This hard hearted man endeavoured to take from him a flageolet he had contrived to make, and which helped to lighten many a weary hour, but the struggle was so agonizing that he thought fit to desist.

A new Governor was appointed to the Bastille in 1764, and greater attention was shewn to the prisoners. Latude had some comforts granted to him to which he had long been a stranger. He sent in memorials and proposed different plans, but his plans were disregarded, and all his pressing solicitations to be brought to trial, or to be

restored to liberty were fruitless. The death of
his father which one of the sentinels communicated
to him seemed to annihilate every remaining hope.
He soon after learned the death of the Marquise
de Pompadour. But he found it was determined
he should continue a prisoner for life.

He was removed after some time to the Château
of Vincennes, and on the 23rd of November 1765
again obtained his liberty in the following daring
manner. He was walking in the Garden attended
by three men when a thick fog came on, he suddenly broke from them, and passed three sentinels.
Another sentinel was stationed at a narrow entrance gate which was fortunately open. He
leaped upon this man and knocked him down and
escaped into the park. He there concealed
himself till the evening and then got into
Paris.

This little interval of liberty was even shorter
than those which had preceded it he was detected
by the Police and restored to his old dungeon at
Vincennes.

The rest of Latude's history during the remainder of his 35 years imprisonment (for with
the short intervals already stated, 35 years elapsed
from the day of his first commitment to the
Bastille to that of his final deliverance) is filled up
with painful details of the miseries endured in a
badly regulated prison. He wrote a letter which
a turnkey promised to deliver, but dropt it in the

street. It was picked up by Madame Le Gros the wife of my French Master. She read with horror the account it gave of the poor prisoner's sufferings copied the letter and forwarded it. She ascertained the truth of the statements, and then devoted herself to obtaining his release. For three years she was incessantly devoted to this object. She sent him all the money she could spare. Weared the public functionaries with applications and the King with memorials, was several times in danger of being shut up herself and after such exertions and zeal as are almost incredible succeeded in obtaining an order for his release. The Government gave him afterwards a small pension as a compensation for his sufferings. Madame le Gros was neither young, pretty or elegant when I saw her ; yet I looked at her with great interest. Latude seemed to idolize her.

Mr. Jackson meets La Fayette, Massena, and Moreau

Francis dined with Mr. —— an American, and came home not well pleased with the party. He met La Fayette and General Massena. The latter is boastful and rough. The command of the Army destined to invade England was given to him and I am told he sometimes talks of it as of a plaything that he could have managed at any time. He abstained from this before Francis, but when

one of the party spoke of the gallantry of 1600
Swiss who defended a pass against 12000 Austrians
Gen. Massena said modestly "I could have cut
my way through it with 30 men."

The character of General Moreau is very different. His courage and skill were attended with
success wherever he directed the forces of the
Republic, and at the same time his mild and
humane conduct ensured him the respect even of
his enemies. The same amiable character attaches
to him here, I consider him to be the most interesting of the whole set. His delicate sense of
honour and justice was recently displayed towards
M. D'Orsin. This Gentleman as an emigrant had
forfeited all his property but has recently been
allowed to return. He was living upon the little
remnants of his wealth. General Moreau sur-
prised him one morning with a visit. After a few
introductory compliments he said, " I have bought
an estate, Sir, which before the Revolution belonged to you. Such property sells very low. I
gave so much for it, I have had it fairly valued,
and the estimate amounts to so much. Allow me
to leave the balance which in justice belongs to
you." He laid down a considerable sum and took
his leave.

A Visit to the Opera Comique

Francis came in the evening to the Opera
Comique, Rue Feydeau ; where Hill and I met

him. It is the prettiest Theatre I have yet seen.[1]
We were well entertained with three very lively
laughable French Operas. Some of the actors
excelled in ease, elegance and humour. I must
confess that the French surpass us in scenic
representations. Yet they were fearfully per-
verted during the Revolution. When the people
were so hardened by continual bloodshed that
they viewed with indifference crouds of their
fellow countrymen dying by the guillotine, they
would go every day from the scaffold to the
theatres, and the conductors of the dramatic
amusements set before them scenes of cruelty and
licentiousness which I cannot relate and which
would have shocked barbarians and savages.

Dec. 12.

I walked with Hill to pay a visit to the lady
who invited us to her dance. We were admitted
and chatted half an hour with a very lively
pleasant woman. On our return we wandered
and lost ourselves. I made an attempt to obtain
some of those beautiful prints of different scenes
in the Revolution and portraits of the men who
were conspicuous in them. But I find it is now
very difficult to procure them. Under the tyranny

[1] The semicircular façade of this building, with gigantic
caryatides between each of its five lofty windows, was certainly
remarkable. It stood in the Rue Feydeau. There is a fine engraving of the Théâtre de l'Opéra Comique by Dubois after
Courvoisier.

I

of Robespierre the houses and shops of artists were subject to domiciliary visits, and if anything which gave offense was found in them the property was destroyed and the owner sent to the guillotine. Many paintings and prints were consequently destroyed which would now be invaluable.

A Novel Stock Exchange

We saw over the door of a fine church the words " La Bourse," and on different parts of the building the words " La Justice," " L'Humanité," and " Liberté." We walked in. The place was crowded with people very like those who frequent our Stock Exchange who were transacting their business in the body of the Church. The Organ remained, so did the old pulpit though its stairs were gone. I observed that most of the persons who entered the door took of their hats for a moment and put them on again. This must have proceded from some lingering sentiment of respect for the place in which their fathers had been accustomed to worship God. I watched the coming in of many, only one missed the salute.

We walked through La Place des Victoires, a handsome oval space in the midst of which stood a large gilt statue of Louis XIV. The buildings surrounding it are uniform and handsome, and were erected as a compliment to the Royal Family. The name still attaches to it. The regal ornaments are all demolished.

Monsieur St. Quintin's Story

You say you like an anecdote. Without further preface I will give you one which was related to Francis of M. St. Quintin, whom he met at a dinner party today. On the 10th of August[1] so remarkable for the siege of the Tuileries St. Quintin was Prefect of the Palace. His friends were all shot round him and he fled from room to room till all chance of escape was at an end unless he would venture to jump from a window of the upper story. It was desperate but he did it and fell upon a heap of dead bodies ; he had recollection enough to lay himself along as if in the same state, and continued there till the evening, when he seized the opportunity which offered of stealing away unnoticed. He went to the house of a stranger, an English woman, who kindly promised to conceal him till he could escape into the country. Some of the mob a few hours after traced him to the house, broke in and began a close examination. The mistress of the house was not out of bed when St. Quintin entered and said it was all over with him, they were searching so closely that escape was impossible. She bade him hide himself in the bed. He had scarcely done so when the ruffians rushed into the room, but they did not perceive him. She spoke to them with great confidence, they looked under the bed, examined every corner,

---

[1] 10 August, 1792.

and then went away satisfied that he was not in the house. He escaped out of Paris in the night and is lately returned.

Traces of the Revolution at the Tuileries

In many parts of the Tuileries is painted in large black letters the words " Le 10 Août." The centre of the edifice was more particularly occupied by the Royal Family, and against that part the cannon of the Republicans were chiefly pointed. Over every hole made by a shot were affixed the words " Le 10 Août." The Government three years ago began to repair the breaches and efface the inscriptions. Some of the fiercer Republicans were offended, and to please them a few of these memorials are left. I was told that I might see a board fixed under one of the windows of the Louvre purporting that " It was from this window the infamous Charles IX fired upon his unfortunate subjects on the Massacre of St. Bartholomew." I looked for it, but it has been recently removed. Horrible as that massacre was, many of the crimes which disgraced the Revolution were as bad.

In the evening we went to the Salle des Étrangers, where a magnificent ball was given by a club consisting chiefly of foreigners. A handsome suite of apartments was open, and about 600 people present. Among them were some very beautiful women, but nine tenths were dressed in a manner which the most profligate females would scarcely venture to adopt. Every other dance was a waltz which seem to give the nymphs and swains opportunities for indulging in freedoms which English modesty would call licentious. I returned home heartily sick of balls.

Anecdotes of Robespierre

Dec. 13.

What a wonderful system of terror was established by Robespierre! And to what an excess of blood thirsty cruelty had the mind of that wretch attained! I have just now heard this anecdote of him. Madame —— ci-devant la Marquise invited Robespierre and Danton to supper. The great men were in good spirits and Robespierre having drank more than usual talked a little too freely. Danton asked him the next morning if he recollected what he had said and repeated something that had escaped him. Robespierre immediately sent an order for arresting every person in the house and in the course of an hour or two, the lady, her husband, three children and several servants lost their heads by the guillotine. In the history of Robespierre's crimes even this appears of no great note. The vengeance of Heaven quickly overtook him, yet even in the agonies of death he continued to inspire terror. On the last morning of his life he had some gloomy suspicions that a storm was hanging over him, and he expressed to his Friend Barrère his wish to avoid going to the Convention. Barrère represented to him that his non-appearance would give his enemies courage and advised him to face the danger. They went to the Convention together, where Barrère himself denounced him and moved the decree for his arrest and trial. Robespierre braved the decree and for some time nobody dared to carry it into effect. He was committed to the Luxembourg Prison, and escaped from thence. He withdrew to the Maison Communale, whence at the head of the Municipality of Paris he issued an edict of outlawry against the Convention. Some troops surrounded the Maison Communale and entered it by storm. Robespierre who was sitting in the hall fell by a musket ball which broke his jaw. Weltering in blood he was laid upon a table without signs of life. A crowd collected round him doubtful whether he was dead. He suddenly recovered himself and sat up. The people round struck with a sudden panic fled from him in all directions as they would have done from a tiger. When he was afterwards carried to the guillotine he was in a weak and apparently dying state.

It will give you some idea of the insecurity of life and liberty under these revolutionary demagogues if you consider the following decree of the Convention denouncing the penalty of death against the enemies of the People. I translate it literally. " And all those shall be esteemed such who seek by force or artifice to destroy Liberty, to debase the National Convention, and the Revolutionary Government of which she is the centre, to mislead the opinion or to hinder the instruction of the people, to deprave manners or to corrupt the public conscience, in a word all those who seek to change the purity of Revolutionary principles."

" The proofs necessary to condemn offenders are every kind of document material or moral, which can naturally procure the assent of a just and reasonable mind."

" The rule for forming Judgments is the con-science of judges enlightened by the love of their country ; their object is the triumph of the Republic, and the ruin of it's enemies. If there exist any documents of the kind abovementioned, no witnesses shall be heard."

" Pleaders or Counsel shall not be allowed except it be for calumniated patriots."

Upon this vague definition of crime, which put life entirely at the disposal of the judge, 322 persons were tried and executed in Paris in eight successive days.

Thermidor, 4 .. 24	7 .. 26	10 .. 22	On this day Robespierre was guillotined.
5 .. 46	8 .. 53	11 .. 70	
6 .. 36	9 .. 45		
		Total .. 322	

Dr. Haygar, a German scholar, dined with us to-day. He has been invited by the French Government to come to Paris, and undertake the completion of a Chinese Dictionary. But on his coming here they offer him only £200 a year and refuse to pay his expenses. He is a talkative entertaining man of 52 or 3, and has just married an English lass of 22.

[Under the dates Dec. 10, 12, and 13 there are some very interesting entries in the diary of George Jackson. He speaks of his brother's resolution to give two official dinners weekly, the first of which had passed off *à merveille*. Rumours of conspiracy are in the air, and certain persons (one fair lady in particular) have endeavoured to induce him to convey certain information to his brother. The First Consul had put off his projected visit to Lyons, to the great mortification of Talleyrand.]

Dec. 14.

Francis gave a magnificent dinner to-day to Lord and Lady Mountcashel,[1] Lord and Lady Cahir,[2] General[3] and Mrs. Pigot etc. I was highly entertained with the first mentioned Lady and her friend Miss Wilmot.

A Visit to the Palace of the Corps Legislatif

Dec. 15.

I endeavoured in my walk this morning to get

[1] Stephen Moore, second Earl Mount Cashel [1770–1822], married 1791 Margaret, eldest daughter of Robert, second Earl of Kingston.   [2] See *ante*, p. 49.

[3] General Sir Henry Pigot.   Commanded at the blockade of Malta in 1800.

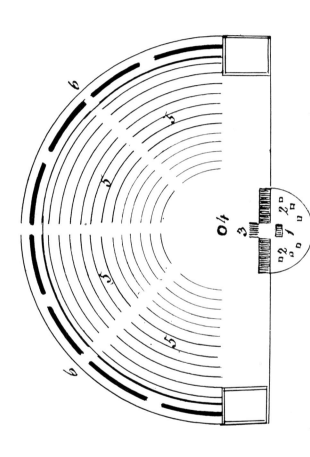

GROUND-PLAN OF THE HALL IN WHICH WERE HELD THE MEETINGS
OF THE LEGISLATIVE BODY IN 1801–2

MADE BY REV. DAWSON WARREN

into the Palace of the Corps Legislatif but was twice refused admittance by the centinels. I spoke to an officer, told him my disappointment, and shewed him my Billet de Sureté, which I had trusted would introduce me. " Ah, Monsieur vous êtes Anglais, J'ai des amis en Angleterre, J'aime les Anglais," and he took me in with the greatest politeness, and gave me an excellent seat. I give you something like a plan.

1. The seat of the President.
2. Six Secretaries of State.
3. The tribune whence the orators speak.
4. L'Autel de la Patrie.
5. Seats for 300 members.
6. Seats for spectators.

It is an excellent room for speaking. There were 281 members present, because it was an interesting question. They were assembled to adopt or reject the first part of a great Constitutional Code of Civil Laws.[1] Les Membres de Corps Legislatif were never allowed to speak, or even to ask a question for information. They enact or reject the Laws proposed to them by the Government, but they can neither propose nor alter. Yes or No is the whole extent of their power. And they pretend to say that this assembly of dumb senators is an improvement upon our House of Commons. The man who invented and established this new species of Legislation thought he could manage his silent puppets as he pleased, but

[1] See *ante*, p. 53.

he is mistaken. A Law was proposed to them on Monday. The President read the Projet. The orators of the Government spoke on its behalf. The subject was the mode in which the laws should be promulgated, and the time after their promulgation at which they should become binding on the citizens. The business had been discussed and settled in the Council of State at which Bonaparte presided. The debate was adjourned till today (Tuesday). When I entered the hall the last orator of the Senate was speaking against the law. He spoke so badly that he excited very little attention. I could only just make out that he was delivering objections against it. When he had finished the President rose and said " The debate is closed." He then asked if they would proceed to the Ballot. They all rose from their seats in token of approbation. One of the messengers brought two urns of green edged with gold and placed one on each side of the tribune. A secretary took his station at one corner of the tribune with a list of the members, and called them over distinctly. As soon as he heard his name each member walked to the tribune, and received from the messenger a black and white ball. He then ascended the steps, and if he approved the law expressed his " Yes " by putting the white ball into the left hand urn. The other urn received the remaining ball. When this was finished another secretary brought two baskets and placed them

The Altar of the Country
the Words on the Book are in gold letters

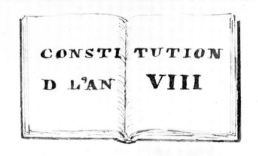

THE ALTAR OF THE COUNTRY

by the urn in front which contained the yeas. He counted over the balls one by one, dividing the white from the black, they amounted together to 281. He then took another basket and counted into it the black balls. When he came near the end there was a dead silence, and the interest seemed to be intense. When he pronounced 142 some of the members could not conceal their joy but burst into plaudits. This was instantly repressed by the authoritative voice of the President echoed by sundry men who appeared to be sentinels who stood in different parts of the hall. The white balls were then counted and found to be 139. The President rose, repeated the numbers and said " The Law is rejected." They then proceeded to other business and I came away.

This is the first time the Corps Legislatif has ventured to reject a law of Bonaparte's. It might have shaken his power had they chosen some popular object on which to express their opposition, but they have foolishly thrown out a measure tending so manifestly to the public good that they will only bring contempt upon themselves and probably strengthen the hands of him whom they meant to oppose.

A party of Englishmen dined here today among whom was Gilliess,[1] whom Francis invited because

---

[1] Gilliess was an excellent scholar, and distinguished himself by his talents and accomplishments. While at Cambridge, he loaded a brace of pistols and he took them out in his pocket for the purpose of practising at a mark. A carter on the road, mis-

he had called upon him.   Gilliess married a French Woman and settled here shortly after the unfortunate affair, which led him to quit England.

Dec. 16.

Called on Mr. Blaquiere who had promised to shew me a collection he had been making in Paris of drawings and etchings.   I lost all credit as a connoisseur by not discovering the merits of some sketches valued highly by the owner but which appeared to me very poor.

Francis, Hill and myself went in the evening to the Opera Buffa, a very elegant theatre but it afforded me no amusement probably because I did not understand Italian.

Dec. 17.

The absolute influence of Bonaparte over the Army must give him very great power added to which the Consuls have a Consular Guard of 3000 men whose pay and privileges are superior to the rest of the Army and who are always on duty at the Tuileries.   How stable the Government will prove time only can shew.   My good wishes attend it.   I think it beneficial to France and by no means an object of dread to England.

taking him it is supposed for another gownsman, struck him two or three times with his cart-whip and wounded him severely in the face.   Gilliess drew a pistol from his pocket and shot him dead. The Coroner's inquest, and the verdict of a Jury acquitted him, but he could not recover his peace of mind in England and went abroad.—D.W.

Dec. 18.

The whole day occupied in sending off a Messenger. I determined to write some thing every day. I can do no more than insert the date.

At the Botanical Gardens

Dec. 19.

Francis, Hill and myself went to the Jardin des Plantes. The Professor was out and we occupied the time before his arrival by looking at the wild beasts, a collection which though national is not equal to the Exhibition over Exeter Change.[1] There is one very fine lion, into whose den the keeper went, put his hands between the jaws to open them, and took up his feet to shew them. Two little cubs a few months old occupied another den, the keeper played with them and invited us to partake in the amusement but we declined the hazardous pleasure. Another lion had a dog for his companion who at his master's command placed himself between his royal patron's paws. We were also entertained by seeing two fine elephants eat their dinner. We walked through some fine conservatories the plants in which I admired without any botanical knowledge of their merits and value. The garden which is spacious and in good order did not at this season of the year

[1] In the Strand. This menagerie continued to exist until the year 1829, when Exeter Change (founded about 1676) was demolished to make way for the improvement of the thoroughfare.

display many of its beauties. We looked into the amphitheatre, a very good building well adapted for lectures. The anatomical subjects forming part of the Museum were the next objects of our attention. It seemed to be a very fine collection, beautifully arranged, and mostly under glass cases. It began with the human brain and there was a series of the brains of other animals down to the Mouse, so that their different conformations were obvious at a glance. The Professor told us it was the finest school of comparative anatomy in the world. The skeletons and limbs appeared innumerable. In another building is preserved a fine cabinet of Natural History. I need not however give an imperfect catalogue. Among the Petrifactions is a block of stone which was sawn in half. The saw cut through a fish like an eel which must have been caught probably by a submarine volcano in the very act of swallowing another and which appeared to have stuck by the way. The bones fins and every part were as plain as in a fresh caught animal. The Museum has been greatly enriched, indeed almost formed from the plunder of other countries. At the end of most of his descriptions the Professor said this specimen came from such a Museum or such a collection from which the powers of General Bonaparte had brought it.

ton pénétré, Adieu, vous voulez donc me faire mourir." The actors placed his bust upon the stage, crowned it with laurels, and recited verses upon his " gloire eternelle."

He died 4 or 5 weeks after this. The archbishop of Paris forbade his burial with the rites of the Church. All Paris was excited, and a decree of the National Assembly in conformity with the wishes of the people appointed a public funeral in the Pantheon.

Louis XVI hurled from the throne of his ancestors was a prisoner in the Tuileries. An officer of the Municipality went to the place where the body of Voltaire had been deposited to carry the decree into execution. The ceremony of his translation was performed with a pomp " aussi majesteuse que piquante."

The removal of Voltaire's remains was attended with every circumstance which could render it majestic and interesting. The procession was headed by the municipal officers in full dress. Numerous corps of Nationals bore on their muskets branches of oak and laurel. A soft and rural band of musick played appropriate airs. Fresh crowds of citizens met the procession at every place, strewing the road with flowers, and offering the choicest garlands. Who can paint the affecting scene ? etc. etc. etc. The roads had been repaired, and triumphal arches erected on the great occasion. Even the ecclesiastics mingled in the civic procession ; like the priests of Apollo they came to chaunt their hymns to the God of Taste as he travelled to his temple. The lofty car which bore him was half pastoral and half triumphal. At the corners rose four pilasters of white marble ornamented with tasteful drapery and garlands of flowers. They were surrounded by a canopy, over which waved the national colours. Between them hung the sarcophagus decked with ribbons and with roses. The space around it was shaded by branches of poplar, cypress beech and elm. Before the car appeared,

" Aux Mânes de Voltaire."

on one side

" Si l'homme est créé libre il doit se gouverner."

and on the other

" Si l'homme a des tyrans, il doit les détrôner."

The horses were covered with violet-coloured trappings and drapery over which bloomed innumerable flowers. When they arrived in a city or town, parties of young damsels clad in white and ornamented with flowers came to meet them bearing crowns or baskets from which they cast a shower of roses, amaranth and jesamine. Then to the sound of the bagpipe or the hautboy they danced around the car. With such religious enthusiasm did David dance before the Holy Ark. Thus did the Graces form their cadenced step, and play before the car of Apollo.

O Voltaire did not thy spirit feel this etc. etc.
He received every where—"les honneurs suprêmes.
C'etoit par-tout la même idolatrie." I imagine
you turning with disgust from this blasphemous
folly. On their arrival in Paris they deposited
the sarcophagus in a pavilion constructed on the
site of the Bastille, amidst the sound of musick
and the shouts of thousands.

The next morning all Paris was congregated.
The boulevards were not wide enough for the
Procession. The gardens windows and roofs of
the houses were crowded with spectators. A
large body of cavalry led the way. The pioneers
of the different battalions bore their axes. The
youths of the military schools. The National
Guards. All the different clubs and societies
of Paris, one of which armed with pikes was called
"Bonnets de Laine." The conquerors of the
Bastille bearing a town flag, the standard of
the late Governor. The widows of those men who
had fallen in the cause, one of them was very
remarkable, she had fought and been wounded,
she was almost ready to give an infant to the
world, yet she bore in her hand a naked sabre.
The deputations of the Provinces in the neighbourhood of Paris each bearing a banner in-
scribed with some verse from Voltaire's writings.
A woman bearing a pike on which was written
"La dernière raison du Peuple." Under rich
canopies were carried the Busts of Descartes,

Rousseau and Mirabeau. Persons dressed in
the characters and carrying the emblems of
History, Poetry, Philosophy, the Muses etc.
A splendid edition of Voltaire's works in a gold
box. Voltaire's statue borne by several men in
long gowns. The actors of the different theatres
in characters. The judges, ministers, Members
of the National Assembly. The ambassadors of
Foreign Powers. A large band of musicians and
singers. "Suivait enfin le Char et la présence
réelle de celui que l'on plaçait en quelque sorte au
rang des Dieux." The car rolled upon four wheels
of bronze, twelve ballustrades formed the spokes,
the fellies were decorated with rosettes and lions
heads etc. A sarcophagus of oriental granite
enclosed the remains of the poet. On each side
were genii weeping with inverted torches and
suitable inscriptions. On the platform were
four antique candelabra on which they burnt
incense and perfumes. Over the sarcophagus
was a couch on which was placed in a reclining
attitude an exact figure of Voltaire. It was covered
with a purple cloth. Immortality under the figure
of a young female seemed to descend from Heaven
and place upon his head a crown of stars. The car
was drawn by twelve white horses. They were
harnessed four abreast and lead by grooms in
Roman dresses. The first pause was at the opera
house. The actors came out and presented garlands etc. with religious enthusiasm. The pro-

of eighty young persons who may be in that
unfortunate predicament. The establishment is
under the jurisdiction of the Minister of the
Interior. Children of the poor under the age of
12 are admitted boarded and taught to read write
and calculate. If the parents can afford it they
pay 600 francs per annum. If not the children
are kept and taught gratuitously. The buildings
are in a bad state. The room in which we were
assembled was small low and crowded. It was
a public day. These circumstances of course
did not lessen the interest my mind had taken in
favour of this humane institution but I was not
pleased at the appearance and contrivance in
the exhibition. It lessened the effect. I could
not help thinking that the pupil whose acquire-
ments were displayed was particularly prepared
to deliver his answers. Yet it was very interesting and occupied us two hours and a half. The
Abbé Sicard[1] (who succeeded the celebrated
de l'Epée) discoursed on the manner and difficulties of instructing the Sourds-muets, and exemplified his remarks by displaying the acquire-
ments of Massieu one of his pupils. The principal
question to be proposed was, What is Galvanism?

[1] The Abbé Roch Amboise Cucurron Sicard [1742–1822].   In
1791 the Constituent Assembly adopted his establishment for
the instruction of the deaf and dumb as a national institution.
He escaped the fate which befell so many of his colleagues almost
by a miracle and was restored to his labours by the Revolution
of 18 Brumaire.   See also *Letters and Journal* of Miss Berry,
Vol. II, p. 162.

L

After stating this, the Abbé gave us a long speech. He prefaced it by apologizing to his audience for going over again some of his former ideas. He did so in compliment to some distinguished strangers who visited him this morning. He proceeded to point out the distinction between those persons who were deaf and consequently dumb from their infancy, and those who had become deaf by any accident or illness. The instruction of the former was a work of great difficulty for he had not only to teach them to express but also to conceive ideas ; the latter had only to acquire a new mode of expressing what they already thought. The latter were therefore of course instructed to form an alphabet by signs and soon gained the power of conversing with those who were acquainted with such signs, but with the former a more circuitous process was necessary. A kind of name was to be given to every object and to every action by some sign which might correspond with it as nearly as possible. He made signs to Massieu and asked What is electricity ? Massieu wrote the question with chalk on a large black frame, and underneath it his answer. This was corrected by the Professor who told him it was " a species of fire." On giving him the word " species " he took occasion to point out the great difficulty of communicating abstract ideas, and by this word he exemplified his mode of teaching very ingeniously. He exercised him in many other ways and at last gave him by common signs the word galvanism. Massieu immediately wrote down what he had read in a journal of an Italian physician named Galvani[1] who had discovered a species of electricity which possessed peculiar properties and which was excited by bringing different metallic plates into contact in a particular manner. A man in the crowd then rose and gave us a long account of this newly discovered fluid. He spoke so low that I lost much of what he said. M. Sicard closed by saying " La Séance est Levée."

On coming out we were invited to look at a young savage caught two or three years ago in the woods of Aveyron. He seemed a stupid boy neatly dressed, and as soon as the door was opened showed an inclination to get out. He had been first taken by three huntsmen as he was climbing a tree, and by them put under the care of a widow. He soon escaped from her, and wandered in the woods and mountains during a most severe winter with very little covering. He then of his own accord entered a house, where he was secured and from whence he was brought to Paris. This poor being is incapable of any attention except to the immediate objects of his animal wants. He is totally destitute of memory, judgment or even the faculty of imitation, for he cannot after months' careful instruc-

[1] Aloisio Galvani of Bologna [1737–1798].

tion be taught to open a door. He never shows the least appearance of curiosity or of thought either by sound or gesticulation. There are many scars on different parts of his body. A large one is conspicuous upon his throat as if it had been made with a sharp instrument, and this leads some to suppose that an attempt had been made to murder this child in the wood, and he had been preserved by the care of some wild beast. In the neighbourhood where he was found he had been seen occasionally running about for 5 years. I thought I saw one of our species either not completely formed or whose faculties had been injured by accident. The savants of Paris imagine that they behold man in his primeval state before he had acquired the use of language.

A Dinner at the British Ministry

Francis gave a splendid dinner to-day to Mesdames Brinola,[1] Morand, Semonville and Jou-

---

[1] Madame la Comtesse de Brignoles (Countess Brinola) was by birth an Italian and the mother of the Piedmontese diplomatist Antoine de Brignoles. She was during the winter 1801–2 a frequent guest of Mr. Francis James Jackson at the Palais Caraman. Miss Berry mentions her under the date 26 March, 1802, as being present with Madame de Staël and other ladies at one of the parties given in the ground floor occupied by the British Minister in the Rue St. Dominique. In 1810 Madame de Brignoles became lady-in-waiting to the Empress Louise, and accompanied her to Vienna, where she died in 1816. Madame de Brignoles was born at Pisa and married at Genoa. Besides her son the Marquis de Brignoles, she had two daughters, the Duchesse

bert[1] the Gentlemen were Lord W. Bentinck,[2] Lord Coleraine,[3] the Swedish Minister etc. We sat down fourteen, but I do not recollect anything particular that may bear recording. We went in the evening to Madame Freville a daughter of Francis's old Spanish Friend Las Heras. There was a large party to whom Texier read a French comedy. It was over about 12 and we were then called to play a Spanish game which consisted in writing the name of a gentleman, the name of a lady and the chance which awaited them. They were then mingled together, and drawn out. The three billets which came together were to be inseparable during the next year. Madame Récamier [4] was to be my partner according to this lot.

[The Vicar of Edmonton seems to have ended the eventful year 1801 as the partner of Madame Récamier in the Spanish game of which we hear

de Dalberg and the Comtesse de Marescalchi. She was a woman of singular ability. More information about the Comtesse de Brignoles will be found in Bausset's *Mémoires,* Tome III, p. 117, and in *Napoléon et Marie Louise,* Tome II, p. 238.

[1] See *ante,* pp. 67, 68.

[2] Lord William Cavendish Bentinck [1774–1839], second son of the third Duke of Portland. In 1801 Lord William Bentinck had been serving with the Austrian forces. Two years later (1803) he became Governor of Madras, and between 1833 and 1835 was Governor-General of India.

[3] An elder brother of the eccentric George Hanger, who declined to assume the title when Lord Coleraine died in 1816.

[4] Jeanne Françoise Julie Adélaïde Récamier, *née* Bernard [1777–1849]. A very interesting biography of Madame Récamier by M. Joseph Turquan has recently been published.

too little. Under these circumstances one must turn for political information to the diary of the young attaché. On Dec. 31 George Jackson says nothing of the party, but writes :—

"The journey to Lyons was again put off ; the 6th and 7th of January is now named for the First Consul's departure. . . . A circumstance connected with these frequent postponements has caused much amusement. The expenses of the journey were calculated at four millions of livres, and that sum was applied for : Barbé Marbois, the minister of public treasure, firmly refused the advance. The First Consul waxed furious, but Barbé Marbois, up to the present, remains firm."]

1802

[Before resuming the thread of the Dawson Warren diary, it will be well to note the course of events during the first month of the New Year, for the expedition to Lyons had far-reaching consequences, destined in the near future to finally interrupt the friendly relations now established between England and France. On 9 January Bonaparte left Paris for Lyons, where he arrived two days later. On 25 January he was elected President of the Italian Republic by the Consulta, and accepted the proffered dignity on the following day. When he returned to Paris on the last day of the month Dawson Warren's sojourn in Paris had terminated.]

The New Year in Paris

January 1, 1802

I heartily wish many happy New Years to you and all my dear friends in England, whom I long to see again. Old customs preserve a great sway over the minds of men in spite of new laws. That natural and innocent one of greeting the New Year is not forgotten here at this season, though the present Calendar begins the year on the 23rd of September. All the confectioners shops are dressed out most gaily and filled with bonbons ; and the ladies spend no small portion of the day in cracking them and reading the mottoes. Had I met with any good ones I would have sent them to you, but all which have fallen in my way are sheer nonsense. M. Erskine [1] the Pope's Nuncio was one of Francis's dinner party yesterday. I ought to have mentioned him before because I conversed a good deal with him and found him very pleasant. He has been lately raised to the rank of Cardinal. In talking of the Republican Calendar he expressed his entire conviction that it will shortly be abolished.

---

[1] Charles Erskine, b. at Rome 13 Feb., 1753, of Scotch Jacobite parents. His brilliant success as a lawyer induced Pius VI to make him a prelate and canon of St. Peter's. After the French Revolution he was entrusted with a mission to London, where he remained eight years. After the Peace he was raised to the rank of a cardinal. He died in 1811. Miss Berry speaks of meeting him in the salon of Madame de Luçay, wearing the costume of a monsignor, as he was still only a cardinal *in petto*.

I took a long walk this morning into the Faubourg St. Antoine, and passed by the Place de la Bastille without knowing it. I looked into the Church of St. Gervais, a handsome building, stripped of all its magnificence and valuables. Here and there a piece of old tapestry is fixed up where formerly was a statue or a painting. Some of the finest paintings taken from this Church are now in the Gallery at the Louvre. I called to enquire after Mrs. Gilliess, she had a fine boy the other day and I am requested to christen it. I hardly know what is my duty. The mother a Roman Catholic and the three sponsors not knowing a word of English. M. Feyteau in whose house Gilliess occupies apartments is a fine old man. He has preserved his fortune through the Revolution without flying the country. He told me that at one time an order was out for arresting him. He knew that to be equivalent to an order for his execution. He escaped out of Paris and walked 60 Leagues to an estate where he thought he was not personally known. But he was recognised, and it soon became the cause of a tumult. One of his carters came into his room in great haste. " Sir it is all over with you ; here are a hundred men coming and swearing they will murder you, they know you are in the house. What can we do ? You had better put on my frock, and go and sit by the kitchen fire." He followed the advice. The men soon came in, searched the house and stood talking about him never suspecting that the object of their search was close by them in a carter's frock.

The Deserted Island on the Seine

The Island of St. Louis is full of very beautiful Hotels, now deserted or let for a trifle. Grass is growing in the streets. It was formerly the residence of many great families. Gilliess took me into an Hotel[1] which must be one of the most superb in Paris. The exterior is fine, built by the architect who raised the Louvre. The apartements are wonderfully rich. A gallery painted by Le Brun and displaying the labours of Hercules, and most splendidly ornamented in every part is said to be one of the finest things in the world. But it is all going to ruin. The wet is coming through the ceilings ; neglect and damp are everywhere visible. The owner is ruined by the Revolution and would be glad to let it for a mere trifle. I had no idea of such desolation and misery as stare upon you in every part of the Isle of St. Louis. Gilliess walked with me part of my way home and just pointed out a church St. Nicholas des Champs now consecrated to " Hymen," and a public House close to it with the sign of " L'Être Suprême."

[1] This hotel formerly belonged to the President Lambert.—D. W.

An Irish Bon-Vivant

I was obliged to hasten home and dress to accompany Francis to a dinner given by Mr. O'Bryne, an Englishman because he was born in Ireland, who seemed to think a good bottle of wine the summum bonum of human life. I was thoroughly sick of this fellow before his dinner was over, though it was a very good one, and I equally disgusted him by telling him I never drank more than a glass or two of wine Somebody had told him I was a celebrated bonvivant. The Prince de Nassau, the çi-devant Duc de Noailles,[1] the Duc de Laval,[2] Lord Coleraine,

[1] Noailles (Louis Marie, Vicomte de), second son of the Marshal de Mouchi, b. in Paris 17 April, 1756, d. 9 Jan., 1804. Served in America under Lafayette. Took the popular side in the Revolution and voted for the abolition of feudal rights and the privileges of the nobility. After suffering a defeat in May, 1792, at the hands of the Duc de Saxe-Teschen he retired, first to England, and then to the United States. He returned to France after the Terror, and was sent to S. Domingo in 1803 with the rank of Brigadier-General. He was mortally wounded in a naval action off Havana. His son Louis Joseph Alexis, Count de Noailles [1785–1833], left France in 1811 and served in the army of the Allies in the campaigns of 1813 and 1814. He held high office under Louis XVIII and Charles X, but went over to Louis Philippe. His brother Alfred, born in 1786, was killed 28 Nov., 1812, in crossing the Beresina.

[2] The Duc and Duchesse de Laval both mentioned by Mr. Warren were not husband and wife, but merely relations. Anne Alexander Marie Sulpice Joseph de Montmorency-Laval, Duc de Laval [1747–1817] resided in the Rue St. Dominique, and according to the police reports of 1802 his house was the scene of constant intrigues against Bonaparte. He was subsequently exiled, but through the influence of his brother-in-law, the Senator de Luynes, he soon obtained permission to return to Paris. His son [1768–1837] was also well known in English society during

Perrégaux and ourselves formed the party. A little while before it broke up the conversation became very interesting. It turned on various events of the Revolution. They spoke in the highest terms of the conduct of the Queen of France in the latter part of her life. Her conduct on the scaffold was peculiarly firm and dignified. The Duke of Orleans was tried at 11 o'clock in the morning, sentenced at two and executed at 4.

Went in the Evening to Madame Roxante's,[1] a French party, and to Lady Cahir's an English party. Nothing very delightful in either.

A Digression on the Progress of Infidelity

Jan. 2nd.

A very fine day. I have availed myself of it by taking a long walk about the City but met with nothing new. The inscriptions on many houses and all the public buildings, " Unité,"

the years 1801 and 1802. He was also an habitué of the salon of Madame Récamier. Catherine Jeanne Tavernier de Boullongne, Duchesse de Laval and Vicomtesse de Montmorency-Laval, lived in the Faubourg St. Honoré. There is an amusing description of her abode in the journal of Madame de Cazenove d'Arlens (Feb.–April, 1803). Her *mauvaise langue* never spared the " great little man," whom she mercilessly ridiculed. She had been a mistress of Talleyrand, but when Bonaparte compelled his Foreign Minister to marry Madame Grand, Louis de Narbonne succeeded him as the lover of the Duchesse de Laval. On 21 March, 1803, Madame d'Arlens writes in her journal : " On frappe. . . . C'est Mme. de Laval, un grand chapeau de paille sur le nez, une petite canne à la main. . . . Elle vieut toute seule et à pied du faubourg St. Honoré. . . ."

[1] See *ante*, p. 129.

" Indivisibilité," etc were put up by order of the Municipality of Paris.

I should like to form a collection of facts which might illustrate the progress of infidelity. We must go many years back to trace the origin of that particular spirit which overturned the ecclesiastical establishment of the country, and in doing so it would be necessary to examine with some attention the progress of literature and manners in France. A very interesting work might be formed from such materials. Very early in the Revolution the clergy gave up their estates and tithes to the state. In 1792 every clerical distinction of dress was prohibited. The respect which had been always paid to Sundays and Saints-days was in the following year expressly forbidden and punishments threatened to those shopkeepers who should venture to express it by shutting up their shops. Shortly after this Gobel, the Archbishop of Paris, accompanied by his vicars-general and several of his clergy appeared in the hall of the Convention and publicly declared that they threw aside their ecclesiastical functions and would in future perform no worship but that of Liberty and Equality. It was about the same time that the Convention by a solemn and public decree declared that there was no God, and that death was only an eternal sleep. With unaccountable inconsistency they soon after made a God or rather a Goddess ;

for at the end of the year 1793 they decreed that the Metropolitan Church of Nôtre Dame should be from that time called and considered " The Temple of Reason." This new divinity personified by an actress and prostitute was attended to her temple by the Convention and all the authorities of the state in public procession. There they placed her on a pedestal and paid their homage with the greatest pomp, singing hymns to her praise. All Christian worship was then entirely suspended, and the Churches became barracks and magazines or temples to some heathen deity or personified virtue. But they were all ordered to be shut up from Christian worship. Notre Dame fut consacrée a la Raison, and L'Eglise des Invalides au Dieu Mars. When afterwards some degree of Public Worship was permitted to be used, the following Churches were allowed :—

EDIFICES RESERVÉS À L'EXERCISE DES CULTES DANS
CHAQUE ARRONDISSEMENT.

Arr.	l'Eglise	consacrée
I.	St. Philippe de Roule ..	à la Concorde
II.	St. Roch	au Genie
III.	St. Eustache	à l'Agriculture
IV.	St. Germain l'Auxerrois	à la Reconnoissance
V.	St. Laurent	à la Vieillesse
VI.	St. Nicholas des Champs	à l'Hymen
VII.	St. Mery	au Commerce
VIII.	St. Margueritte	à la Liberté & a l'Egalité
IX.	St. Gervais	à la Jeunesse
	Nôtre Dame	à l'Etre Suprême

   X. St. Thomas d'Aquinas   à la Paix
  XI. St. Sulpice . . . . à la Victoire
 XII. St. Jacques de Haut-pas à la Bienfaisance
       St. Medard . . . . au Travail
       St. Etienne de Mont . . . à la Pieté Filiale

For on the 18th of Floreal year 2[1] they passed
a decree that there was a God, and that the
human soul was immortal; and they held a
Fête à L'Etre Suprême; and the above Churches
as they had not been applied to secular purposes
were allowed to be opened for divine service.
At first crouds poured in, but the novelty was
soon over and indifference returned. I fear this
indifference is very general, for they seem to
think that the great use of religion is to serve
as an auxiliary to government. It is under this
idea, and because he thinks it will be politically
useful that Bonaparte is now meditating its
restoration.

    Francis took Hill and myself to Madame
de la Rochefoucauld[2] a lady of the old Court.
There was a party of çi-devant Ducs, Viscomtes
et Princesses. It was not quite to my taste,
probably because they took very little notice
of me. We staid late and at eleven tea and
supper were brought in together.

   [1] Wednesday, 7 May, 1794.
   [2] The widow of Duke Louis Alexandre de la Rochefoucauld,
who at first showed some sympathy with the reform movement.
His disapproval of the conduct of Péthion and Manuel in 1792
made him obnoxious to the Jacobins and he was assassinated at
Gisors in Sept., 1793. He was then sixty.

Walks, Dinners and Visits

Jan. 3

Sunday.   Eight or nine only attended our service.   The river was higher than ever known on account of a canal bursting its banks.   Francis and I in walking out were forced to avail ourselves of a boat to go the length of a street.   The frost is set in exceedingly severe.   I never suffered so much from cold as today.

Jan. 4

Very bad weather.   Francis gave a dinner to several Englishmen.   Sir Robert Barclay, Mr. Tyrwhitt, M.P. for Okehampton, La Heras etc. Mr. Tyrwhitt said he was in Paris when the Margravine[1] of Anspach passed through it.   She gave a great deal of trouble which exposed her to some marks of rudeness from Bonaparte. She asked him if she might travel through the country and cross the water under the protection of the neutral flag.   He replied : " Pray go quietly and be satisfied that people know nothing about you and your neutral flag."   At another time she was paying a visit to Madame Bonaparte. The Consul entered the room, spoke to two or three people, passed her by and departed abruptly.

In the year VI[2] all good Citizens were required

---

[1] See *The Beautiful Lady Craven*, by A. M. Broadley and Lewis Melville.   John Lane.   In this book will be found a long and interesting letter addressed to Mr. Francis James Jackson in 1802, when English Minister Plenipotentiary at Berlin.

[2] 1798.

to take this oath. "I swear to be faithful to the Nation, to maintain Liberty and Equality or to die in their defense." The priests who had made themselves constitutional by taking this oath, and were consequently allowed to celebrate divine service assumed a right of electing their own Bishops and exercised it particularly in the Department of the Seine. The Parisians continued after this to dedicate temples and build altars to the heathen gods and goddesses especially upon their public Fêtes. A decree was issued at the end of the year VI commanding the shops to be shut and all reverence to be paid on the Decadis and National Fête-days, and that no marriages should be celebrated but on the Decadi.

[Neither Mr. Dawson Warren, nor Mr. George Jackson mention the marriage of Louis Bonaparte and Hortense Beauharnais, which was celebrated on 4 Jan. in the chapel of the Tuileries. The ceremony was performed by Cardinal Caprara and Bonaparte was present.]

Mr. Jackson officially received by the First Consul

Jan. 5 [1]

This being the day of the second public parade and audience since our residence in Paris, and the first since Francis received his credentials, we expected a notice to attend the Chief Consul.

[1] This somewhat important audience has entirely escaped the notice of M. Albert Schuermans. See *Itinéraire*, p. 124.

BONAPARTE IN 1801-2

FROM A CONTEMPORARY ENGRAVING PURCHASED BY REV. DAWSON
WARREN DURING HIS STAY IN PARIS

None came till one o'clock. This was afterwards accounted for as an omission of one of the officers. We entered the Court of the Tuileries a few minutes before two. Francis wore a full Court dress, Hill the regimentals of the Shropshire Militia, and I my canonicals. My gown attracted a great deal of attention both out of doors and after we had entered the Hall where the Corps Diplomatique were assembling. One of the Ambassadors asked Francis if he always travelled with a confessor, and another asked him if I was a monk. Such a thing as a clerical habit had not been seen in Paris for many years. We waited in this Hall walking about and conversing till the Ministers and their suites had arrived, and till the first Consul was ready to receive us. During that time coffee, chocolate and other refreshments were handed round. At length an Aide-du-Camp announced that the Chief Consul was ready to receive us, the folding doors were thrown open, and we walked upstairs. Grenadiers in the rooms and on the staircase formed lines through which we passed. Officer's Guards were stationed in the antirooms ; drums beat, and arms were presented as we approached. Francis and we, as his suite being strangers entered the presence room first, preceded and ushered in by four messengers of state, and the Préfet de Service, a sort of Master of the Ceremonies. It is a very noble apartment very finely painted and richly

M

ornamented. At the farther end, dressed in his full Consular uniform, which I have before described stood

1. Bonaparte, First Consul.
2. Cambacérès, Second Consul.
3. Le Brun, Third Consul.
4. Talleyrand, Barbé-Marbois, & 4 or 5 other Ministers of State.
5. Some other public or other functionaries.
6. Several general officers.
7. Soldiers of the Consular Guard with their hats and Helmets on, fine tall men.

The spectacle was very grand and imposing. They were all motionless, except Bonaparte who fixed every eye upon him by moving a little forward in advance of the rest, where he stood till we were arranged by the officers who had conducted us. Then we stood

8. Francis.
9. Myself.
10. Hill.
11. The Etrurian Minister,[1] for it was also his first introduction.
12. Other Diplomatists with their suits among whom stood.

---

[1] Don Luis of Parma and his wife Maria Luisa Josephine de Bourbon, daughter of Charles IV of Spain, had visited Paris in May, 1801, to thank the First Consul for their nomination to the throne of Etruria. In virtue of the treaty concluded with Spain, France acquired Parma, while Don Luis became King of Etruria (Tuscany).

stove.

7 Line of Grenadiers &c 5 4 4 2 . 1 3 4 4 4 5 5 with Hats & Caps on, armed 7

6 6 6 6 6 6

8 12

9 12

10 12

11 13

12 12 12 12 12

Préfet de
Service
Messengers of State
and
other Attendants

Officers .

Antiroom
with an
Officer's
guard
Drum &c

o o
o o
o o
o o
o o
o o
o o
o o

PLAN OF THE ROOM IN WHICH WE WERE RECEIVED
BY NAPOLEON

13. Mr. Livingston, the American Minister and his Secretary.[1]

As soon as the Circle was formed, Bonaparte walked up to Francis in a graceful manner and the introduction was made by the Préfet de Service. Francis delivered the King's Letter which Bonaparte received with a bend forward which I thought was a bow. He looked at it and then delivered it into the hands of Talleyrand. A little conversation ensued in which the First Consul said the friendship between the two nations ought to be eternal, and they might ensure the repose of the world, to which Francis replied that he had the honour of bearing to France the earnest wishes of his Royal Master and of the British People that it might be so. Bonaparte dropped some remark on the British Government having sent him a very young man, but it was with a good-humoured smile, to which Francis replied with an equal good humour that he was sent to a young man.

Bonaparte and the English Chaplain

After a few words more Bonaparte looked to me. My dress caught his attention. I ad-

[1] Chancellor Robert R. Livingston, Minister Plenipotentiary of the United States to France. The first thing he heard on his arrival in Paris in Nov., 1801, was the news of the cession of Louisiana and the Floridas by Spain to France. Many interesting details about Livingston's mission to France, 1801–3, will be found in Mr. H. W. Dickinson's *Robert Fulton, Engineer and Artist*. John Lane, 1913.

vanced a step or two and Francis introduced me. He gave me a slight bow and asked what costume I wore ? Francis replied " D'un Ecclésiastique bénéficié." The Consul addressed me " Êtes-vous Évêque ? " To which I replied, " Pas encore." By which I only meant to imply I was of inferior rank, but it has drawn upon me some jokes and laughs. Bonaparte then said '' De quel diocèse." " De Londres." " L'Évêque de Londres est un homme de grand mérite."[1] He then turned to Hill " Et vous, Monsieur, quel est votre uniforme ? " " De la milice, Général." " De quel Comté ? " " Shropshire." He then went round the semicircle having something pleasant to say to every body. To the American Minister he was particularly attentive. Mr. Livingston is a deaf old man, and cannot speak a word of French. When his Secretary stated this, the Consul replied " Ce n'est rien, ce n'est pas nécessaire pour parler la langue de la libertè." When he had completed the circuit he returned again speaking to two or three persons a second time. He stopt close to me and said " Êtes-vous Sécretaire de Legation ? " " Non Général," for that is the title by which he expects strangers to address him, his own subjects call him " Citoyen Consul." " Qu'est ce que vous êtes donc ? "

---

[1] The Bishop of London in 1801 was Dr. Beilby Porteus [1731–1808]. He occupied the metropolitan see from 1787 until his death. The Rev. Dawson Warren supplies a lengthy note upon his domestic and episcopal virtues.

" Un ami, et le beau-frere du Ministre." " Êtes-vous Puritan ? " I did not at first understand him not supposing that he could enquire if I was one of a set of men so long ago extinct. On his repeating the question I said " Je suis de l'Église Anglaise." " Anglicaine vous voulez dire—Ah, vous êtes Anglicaine "—His countenance was pleasing and animated. He appeared very different from what I had before thought him to be. His manner was easy and unembarrassed, and he went through the whole ceremony as if he had been accustomed to Courts all his life. When he had had enough of our company, he took his original station between the two Consuls, and made a graceful bow. We all returned in the same order we had entered.

A Squabble about Precedence

In coming out there was a scuffle between the Etrurian Minister and me, he said that he had a right to go first, I replied that he was very welcome, he then said perhaps he had not a right and I answered " Perhaps not." As this caused an interruption there was a cry of " Go on," and I felt somebody's hand upon my shoulder quickening my movements, but which of the two important personages went first I cannot say. As I was getting into the carriage one of the croud assembled at the door said " Voilà une femme qui monte dans la voiture." We immediately paid

visits of compliment to Madame Bonaparte and
the Ministers of the different Departments.

The British Plenipotentiary Dines with the Three Consuls

Francis dined at the Palace.   A very handsome
dinner, to which 220 persons sat down, and all
were accommodated at one table.   My name
was not inserted in the card of invitation by
mistake of the officer ; for Bonaparte asked why
I was not there ?   The Consul was very attentive
to Francis and conversed with him a good deal.
He concluded some remarks on the progress of
the negotiations at Amiens by saying " If the
English make peace as well as they have made
War they will do very well."   The dinner was
rather hurried.   Bonaparte had every now and
then an odd trick of moulding a piece of bread
into a pellet and tossing it into his mouth.   He
always caught it.   A superb dessert was arranged
on the table but the Consul apparently in a fit
of absence rose and said to Francis " Voulez vous
du café ? " and then led the way into the drawing
room where coffee, ices and liqueurs were handed
round, and they soon separated.

[Mr. George Jackson gives a much fuller
narrative of the banquet of which he must have
received a detailed account from his brother.   He
gives the exact number of guests present as 248.
It took place in the great gallery of the Tuileries,

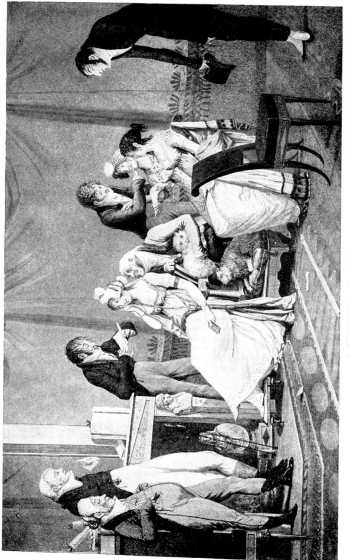

A PARISIAN RECEPTION IN 1801

FROM L. P. DEBUCOURT'S AQUATINT "LES VISITES" PUBLISHED 1 JAN. 1801

and myself plain black. At the door of Cambacérès stood a sentinel and another at the top of the stairs. He is a rough-looking unpleasant man, but he received Francis very politely, and they stood and conversed together for some minutes. A secretary and two officers stood behind him.

A Visit to Le Brun

We found Le Brun,[1] the third Consul a most pleasant and gentlemanlike man. He was alone, and the audience with him differed from a common visit only that he did not ask us to sit down. The consuls were not in full dress which is red embroidered with gold, but in half-dress which is blue. They wore embroidered boots and pantaloons. The titles of Citoyen and Citoyenne are getting quite vulgar and they will soon be out of fashion with the lowest. They say it is now and then used in connection with another as Citoyen Ministre. The Consuls and their functionaries write Monsieur and Madame, so does Madame Bonaparte.

We all to-day dined with Lord Cahir a flat dinner and a cold room.

[1] Charles Francis Le Brun [1739–1824]. Like Cambacérès, Le Brun was a lawyer, and acted as Secretary to the Minister Maupeon. At the Revolution he sat in the States-General, and also in the Council of Five Hundred. Napoleon chose him as the Third Consul, and he was rewarded after the foundation of the Empire with the title of the Duke of Placentia. He was subsequently Governor of Liguria and Administrator-General in Holland. He ended his public career (after the return of the Bourbons) as Grand Master of the University.

Bonaparte's True Character

Jan. 8

Bonaparte's general character is that he disdains flattery, and is unmoved by personal compliments. The papers pour forth adulation in copious streams, which of course he approves of if he does not command ; for the Press is absolutely at his disposal. So it teems with praises of his public administration, his wisdom, genius and courage, and continually acknowledges the infinite obligations he has conferred upon the French nation. I send you a copy of verses which his Consulship was pleased very graciously to receive at the last parade.

Acrostiche présenté au premier Consul à la parade
    du 15 nivose [5 Jan. 1802]
B—oussole des Français, Consul guerrier et sage,
O—bjet de leur amour, accueille mon hommage.
N—os cœurs, depuis la paix, sont heureux et contens.
A— te former, le ciel se prépara long-tems :
P—oursuis, digne Heros, l'on jouit de tes veilles
A—joute chaque jour merveilles sur merveilles.
R—efais l'esprit public, mets unterme aux abus.
T—on nom, couvert de gloire, est beau pour nos
    oreilles.
E—n te voyant de près, on t'admire encore plus.
        Par Puthod (de Mâcon) adjutant-Commandant,
        Ex-membre de la Commission des Arts.

bers of the Directory, Council of Antients and Council of 500 were banished to Cayenne. Barbé Marbois was among these exiles, and suffered much from the inhuman treatment he experienced on the journey. He was locked up with 15 others in an iron cage constructed upon wheels. His companions escaped to England, but he remained at Cayenne above a year, and appeared again on the public stage in the year 8[1] as Counsellor of State. He was raised by Bonaparte who knows his value to his present situation.

Jan. 10.

Sunday. We had again but a thin congregation. We were all quietly at home both at dinner and in the evening.

Story of the Place de la Concorde

Jan. 11.

I set out at 10 for a long walk, and made on foot nearly the whole circuit of Paris. The Place de la Concorde, between us and the Tuileries has changed its name twice as many other places have done. Its monarchical title was Place de Louis XV, the Jacobins called it Place de la Révolution and it gained its present name under a Government which affects to conduct itself upon a system of moderation. It is a large square, surrounded by a great deal of ornamental stone work, and some statues. Its great ornament

[1] 1799.

before the revolution was an equestrian statue
in bronze of Louis XV placed on a lofty pedestal
of white marble. The mob destroyed it, and
on its site was erected the guillotine, by which
they murdered the unfortunate Louis XVI. The
King's body was buried in quick lime that it
might not be afterwards found. Many persons
were sacrificed on the same spot during the Terror.
They were then carried in carts and thrown into
large pits dug in the church-yard of the Madeline.

The Gates of Paris

I walked along the Boulevard, a broad handsome street planted on each side with trees
which separate the road from a wide footway.
This goes from the Madeline and makes a large
sweep round the northern side of the city. The
Porte St. Denis, and the Porte St. Martin are
two triumphal arches which stand across two
streets bearing the same names. Yet not across,
for the roads pass on each side as well as through
them. I passed close by the Temple but saw
little of it. There is not much to see in the exterior
and the interior they will only shew to Prisoners.
Sir Sidney Smith was confined there and escaped
from it. I crossed the Isle St. Louis, and walked
about the Island which formerly contained the
whole city of Paris, but is now an inconsiderable
part of it. At the Palais de Justice I endeavoured
to get into the Courts of Criminal Justice, but the

sentinels refused me admission and persisted in their refusal though I presented my Carte de Sureté and offered a passport generally efficacious, a piece of silver.

The handsome front of the College of Surgeons caught my attention. The nature of the establishment has been changed. The Convention called it L'École de Medecine. Most of the useful institutions of Paris have been new-modelled by the present or late Governments, as if pulling to pieces and putting together again could benefit the community. Perhaps the true motive may be traced in their hatred to their antient monarchy. The munificence of the sovereign had been the great source of these beneficial establishments and the object of the reformers was to efface all recollections of their royal benefactors. Nothing else attracted my notice. But I had not been at home five minutes when Francis invited me to another walk. So you see I shall not be ill for want of exercise. He finds living here very expensive.

A Pleasant Dinner at the Hôtel Caraman

A large party dined with us today, the Caraman family,[1] Lord Aberdeen,[2] and a friend of his,

[1] See *ante*, pp. 55, 81, 82.

[2] George, third Earl of Aberdeen [1784–1860]. He had succeeded to the title on the death of his father during the previous year. He was only eighteen in 1802. Exactly half a century later he became First Lord of the Treasury and Prime Minister of England.

N

and Major Birch.[1] The Major and I met with mutual surprize, not having met since we were together at College. Nor did I know that Francis had been acquainted with him for some time. He has been in very active service in Egypt as chief on the Quarter Master's Staff, he had to reconnoitre the enemy, to plan the encampments, to make such reports and to draw such plans as may enable the Commander-in-Chief to give his orders, and after all he has to lead the columns into the field. Birch is now hastening home to lay his plans etc before the Duke of York, who seems to give the warmest encouragement to talent and industry in the officers of the Army. He had a cruel loss of two large books full of drawings and plans, his first works in Egypt. He gave them in charge of the captain of the ship with whom he had sailed and they have never since been seen. Birch spoke enthusiastically of Sir Ralph Abercromby and represented his attention to business and his kindness to every individual of the Army as wonderful. His courage was a little too vehement for his station ; at the time of landing he would have been in the thickest of the danger which would not have been proper or necessary. His friends therefore had recourse to a little artifice.

----

[1] John Richard Birch, son of John Birch of Tooting, matriculated at Trinity College, Oxford, 14 Oct., 1790, at the age of seventeen.

The Captain of the " Kent " was to carry him on shore. This officer had been removed from the " Veteran " and had taken his old seamen to his new ship, he therefore prepared his boat's crew. " My lads, when I call to you, pull away *veterans*, make a great noise and splashing with your oars but don't pull. When I say pull away *Kent*, then do it in earnest." The General when in the boat saw the other boats making the shore quicker than he did. He was excessively impatient and begged the Captain to quicken the exertions of his men. " Pull away veterans," and the splashing satisfied him. Sir Ralph saw soon after that the landing was effected and that the enemy was retreating from the beach. The Captain then thought it time to yield to the entreaties of the General, and " Pull away Kent " put them on shore presently. The moment he landed he ran after his men, but, being an old man his breath failed him. They brought him a dragoon's horse, as he tried to mount the saddle he turned round and said, " Never mind I am not tired yet " and then rushed on.

I declined going out in the evening, having a violent toothache.

Jan. 12.

Major Birch breakfasted with us, gave us some very entertaining accounts of the expedition to Egypt, and showed us a great many plans and drawings. He then set off on his way to England.

Jan. 13

Francis took George and myself to the Manufactory of Bronze d'Or. Many most elegant
articles, tables, clocks, figures, candelabra etc.
but at extravagant prices. We went afterwards
to the China Manufactory and were still more
pleased. Beautiful biscuit figure clocks and
services of all kinds. One dessert service was
very superior in magnificence, each single plate
costing nine Louis. Finding the clocks to bear
enormous prices, I refrained from purchasing
one. We saw some painting on glass beautifully
executed. The man had recently began and
doubted whether it would pay him.

Some Stories of the Revolution—a Digression

Posterity will scarcely believe the horrors of
the French Revolution, especially that part of
it when the Country was under the Tyranny of
Robespierre and the anarchists. Did you ever
hear of Les Chemises Rouges ? It is a horrible
Tale. You may pass it over, if you cannot
prepare your mind for a story of cruelty and
blood.

Leonard Bourdon was sent to Orleans by
the Convention as their Commissary. Devoid
of all principle and decency, this man was continually immersed in drunkenness and debauchery,
and would often in a state of intoxication, and

Liberté.

Egalité.

Paris, le 21 Nivose an 10.
de la République française.

Le Consul Cambacérès prie
Monsieur Dawson - Warren, de venir diner
chez lui le 24 du courant, à cinq
heures et demie.

Réponse s'il vous plait.

INVITATION SENT BY SECOND CONSUL CAMBACÉRÈS ASKING REV. DAWSON
WARREN TO DINE WITH HIM AT 5.30 P.M. IN JANUARY, 1802

epicure that ever eat. I endeavoured to count the number of dishes of which my two companions partook but I lost the reckoning somewhere about four or five and twenty. Had I known that one of them was Target[1] who refused to plead before the Convention for Louis XVI my disgust would have been greatly increased.

Cambacérès has been an active man in public affairs from the beginning of the Revolution, but he has had the wisdom not to step forward into the first ranks. He was one of the six commissioners chosen by the Convention to prepare the papers for the trial of the King; on which occasion he exerted himself very much. He was one of the Deputation sent to enquire what Counsel the King would appoint. When Target refused to undertake the defense of Louis, Cambacérès fearing that others would be equally intimidated proposed that the Convention should appoint the Counsel and compel them to plead. The necessity of adopting this measure was immediately removed by the spirited offers of men who performed the office they undertook with equal courage and ability. The Speech of Deséze[2] in the defence of his Sovereign is one

---

[1] Guy Jean Baptiste, Advocate, b. 1733, d. 1806. In 1791 he was ridiculed in a pamphlet entitled *Couches de papa Target.* In 1796 he published a defence of his conduct in declining to defend Louis XVI.

[2] Deséze or De Séze was associated with Malesherbes and Tronchet in the defence of the King.

of the most beautiful and eloquent compositions I ever read. Had not the wretches on whom depended the fate of their injured Monarch been predetermined as to their sentence must have saved him. When the Convention had pronounced him guilty Cambacérès urged their immediately proceeding to the sentence, but on its coming to his turn to express his opinion as one of the Judges, he was milder than his colleagues. He thought it would be of service to the Republic to keep him in confinement as a hostage until a general peace, and then to determine on his fate.

From the dinner-table we retired early to the drawing rooms in which a great deal of Company was assembling; as it was the Consul's public night. Even in the magnificent establishment of the Second Consul there are incongruities which offend my English taste. A cook with a paper cap on his head and short apron was now and then putting his head into the dining room and looking round him. Accustomed also to the cleanliness and neatness of an English table, the knives spoons and forks always appear dirty. The brightness of these articles at Francis's dinners always extort admiration, a proof that it is not common. I forgot to tell you one instance of the epicurean attention paid by the Consul to his guests. He called the attention of the party and announced that in order to give them the advantage of eating some souflets in perfection he had ordered an oven to be constructed as close as possible to the dining room, "they are just ready" he said. And after a little pause, the well trained menials set before each guest a something in white paper which we all eat with every possible expression of admiration.

The Vicar of Edmonton meets Notre Dame de Thermidor

We went at 10 o'clock to Mr. Smith an American; a fine house and a great deal of apparently good company. The entertainment was musick. The beautiful Madame Tallien was there. I was disappointed. But as I did not speak to her and was not introduced to her, I must not express an opinion about her.[1]

About the Palais Royal

Jan. 15

I rarely walk out without passing through the Palais Royal. This place has changed its

---

[1] Theresa Cabarrus, afterwards Marquise de Fontenay, Madame Tallien, and finally Princesse de Caraman-Chimay [1773–1835]. The claims of Madame Tallien to the sobriquets of "Notre Dame de Thermidor" and "Notre Dame de Secours," which the traditions of the best part of a century have consecrated, are mercilessly attacked by M. L. Gastine in his remarkable book *Madame Tallien* (John Lane, 1913). It is to be hoped that on 14 Jan., 1802, the ex-Queen of the Convention was not wearing the diaphanous raiment so minutely described by her latest biographer, and which had in turn delighted Barras, Bonaparte, Ouvrard, and many others.

O

name several times. It received from Cardinal
Richelieu who built it the title of Palais Cardinal.
By Louis XIV it was called Palais Royal. The
Jacobins styled it Palais Égalité, and its present
denomination is Palais du Tribunat. It has
two large square courts, and beyond them a
large open space laid out in strait lines and walks.
This is surrounded by houses built in a uniform
and handsome style with piazzas which afford
a sheltered walk. Before the Revolution it was
a centre of attraction for the fashionables of
Paris. They assembled here full-dressed, and
were sure of meeting the most agreable and
elegant company, while the shops offered every
article of taste and fancy. The scene is now
changed. It is a receptacle for all that is vile
of either sex. The fashionable and the noble
are succeeded by thieves and prostitutes who
elbow passengers by day and would plunder them
by night.

A Conversazione at Madame de Staël's

We attended in the evening a party at Madame
de Stael's[1] musick and conversation. I was
amused by conversing with two or three of the
Savants who had accompanied the Expedition
to Egypt.

[1] Madame de Staël, *née* Necker [1766–1817]. No further note
is needed of the gifted woman who figures so constantly and so
conspicuously in the letters and journals both of Madame d'Arblay
and Miss Berry.

Jan. 16

Hill and I walked out to pay visits. First
to Madame de Stael who probably from our
neglect of that little ceremony did not choose
to speak to either of us last night. While we
waited, the man-servant went into her room
and returned to deliver her message that Madame
was extremely sorry she could not see us, Elle
est encore dans son lit, (it was then past one)
but she will be up at four and would be happy
to receive us after that hour. This lady is the
daughter of Necker the great Financier. Gibbon
speaks in high terms of the beauties, graces and
learning of her mother. The first of these en-
dowments certainly does not descend to the
daughter, I have not penetration enough to dis-
cover any of the second, her profession of the
third is vouched for by universal opinion. Hill
said there was a party of men in the room, and
we were contented with leaving our cards. Nobody knows or enquires about her husband.
He is supposed to be a worthless man with whom
she cannot live and that he subsists in obscurity
upon a small pension she allows him.

A Visit to the Invalides

After a long walk we went for the first time to
the Hôtel des Invalides, which we had neglected
doing sooner because it was so near to the Hotel
Caraman that we could do it easily at any time.

The edifice, though not equal to our Greenwich Hospital is a very magnificent building. Before it is a large space open to the river, and fringed with young trees. The Church is a fine object from the opposite banks. Over the gateway, by which you enter a large square court, the Republican cant of " Unité " " Indivisibilité," etc fills the spaces once occupied by the armorial bearings of France, and by this simple and beautiful inscription, " Læso ac invicto Militi." Within the entrance of the building which is now encumbered with the wooden frame work fixed up for the illuminations of the late Fête is put up in large letters, " Içi on s'honore du titre de Citoyen." Louis XIV founded this establishment as a comfortable retreat for the wounded officers and soldiers of his army, 3000 of whom can be accommodated without inconvenience. The building forms a large square, along the sides of which are apartments for the men, and others of a superior kind for the officers. The Church, however, the çi-devant Church for it is now the Temple of Mars, is the great object of attention, and must have been a magnificent place of worship. It stands opposite as you enter the quadrangle.

Rows of pillars and arches running down the whole building divide it into three aisles and support the gallery. From the front of this gallery and from the walls are suspended the

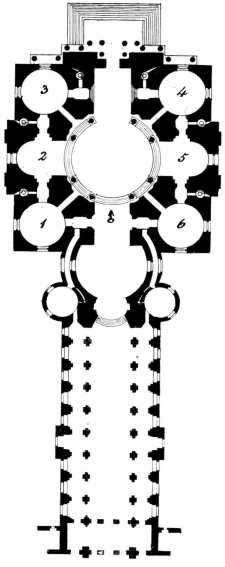

THE INVALIDES IN 1801-2

FROM A PLAN OBTAINED BY REV. DAWSON WARREN

colours taken by the armies of France in the late war. It is a very large collection, though an Englishman must derive great pleasure from perceiving that this monument of national pride is decorated with very few flags taken from his country. In the sanctuary where once stood the high-altar, ornamented with fine bronze statues and glittering with gold is now a plain grecian altar surmounted by a statue of Mars. What a subject for reflection is this that in these enlightened times the idolatry of the old Pagans should triumph over the ruins of Papal superstition. Round the upper part of the altar on which the statue sits, and which is circular, runs a border of antique swords supported by wreaths and underneath each sword is written the name of one of the French Armies. This intimates of course pretty clearly that each army is as a sword in the hand of the heathen god of battles. I took a list of these armies.

Armée du Rhin
Armée de l'Intériure
Armée d'Italie
Armée d'Angleterre
Armée d'Orient
Armée de Danube
Armée de Tyrolie Orientale
Armée d'Ouest
Armée de Sambre et Meause

earth over the floor which laid there two or three
years. Most of the statues were removed to the
Museum of French Monuments. It is curious to
observe that the Roman Catholics had given to
each of the four Doctors two female saints as
associates. I wonder at the want of gallantry
in Frenchmen when they turned them out.
The effect of visiting the Church of the Invalides
in its present state is exceedingly curious. Scrip-
tural subjects, heathen Gods, allegorical personages, and monkish fables are strangely jumbled
together. I am led alternately to laugh at the
folly, to wonder at the versatility, and to pity
the blindness of the people. But the last emotion
prevails, and I earnestly wish that the light of
truth may shine upon them.

Francis gave a dinner today to a party of
Englishmen, Lord Aberdeen etc., Landon[1] of
Oxford was one of the party, a clergyman; he
came here dressed as a layman, but seeing me
appear in clerical costume he laid aside his queue
and reassumed his own character. Vaughan of
All Souls was also here. Went in the Evening to
the Duchesse de Rohan[2] a party chiefly of the

[1] Either James Landon [1765–1850], Worcester College,
Vicar of St. Mary-the-Virgin, Oxford, 1797, or Whittingdon
Landon [1758–1838], also of Worcester College. Vice-Chancellor,
1802–6; Dean of Exeter, 1813–38.

[2] Catherine Frederica Wilhelmina Bénigne Biron, Princess of
Courlande, eldest daughter of the last Duke of Courlande, b.
8 Feb., 1781, d. 28 Nov., 1839. Married 23 July, 1800, Prince
Jules Armand Louis de Rohan, General in the Austrian Army.

ci-devant noblesse. We had not the splendor
and expense of some other houses, but the manners
and dress were much more to my taste than anything I have seen in Paris, and lead me to form
some idea of what Paris was when the members
of her aristocracy were thus polished and refined.
A second room was opened at 11 o'clock for tea,
which consisted besides that beverage of soups,
sweetmeats and fruit.

Jan. 17

A thin congregation again. Only three besides
our own family.

A Mixed Dinner at the Legation

Francis gave a dinner today to a medley
French, Spaniards, Poles Germans and Englishmen. M. de Noailles[1] gave us an anecdote of
General Moreau which is accordant with his
character, and does him credit. When Rewbel[2]
was President of the Directory an infamous

Having been divorced from the Prince de Rohan in March, 1805,
she remarried, two months later, with Prince Basile Troubetzkoi.
After a second divorce she became the wife of Count Charles
Rudolph de Schulenbourg. She was the first to bear the title
of the Duchesse de Sagan. Speaking of her in his letters Reichardt
describes the Princess de Rohan as "the queen of the foreign
colony with an absentee husband." In the *Journal des Débats*
of 22 frimaire, An XI (13 Dec., 1802), is an account of a brilliant
ball given by her at which Lord and Lady Cholmondeley and all
the élite of the English colony were present. She should be
described as Princess and not Duchesse de Rohan.

[1] See *ante*, p. 154.

[2] With Rewbell in 1796 were associated as Directors Barras,
Letourneur, La Réveillière-Lépaux, and Carnot. He is mentioned
in 1803 as one of those who desired the overthrow of Bonaparte.

decree was passed that the French Armies should never give quarter to the English nor to Hanoverians. Moreau was appointed to the command of an Army and Rewbel took an opportunity of charging him to carry into full effect this butchering system but the General replied. " I should have taken no notice of this Decree if you had not mentioned it, but should have done my duty. You now compel me to say that my conduct shall not disgrace the character of a soldier and a Frenchman. You are at liberty to appoint another to the command." To estimate the spirit of such a reply, you must recollect the absolute power of Rewbel at that time.

The Paris Theatre

Jan 18

Went in the evening to the Thèatre Français; stupid enough. A party at General Marmont's,[1] he married a daughter of Perrégaux the banker.

[1] Auguste Frederic Louis de Marmont, Duc de Raguse [1774–1852]. Entered the army in 1789. In 1796 he was first aide-de-camp to Napoleon, when commanding the army of Italy. Was defeated by Wellington at Salamanca. He gave in his adhesion to the Bourbons in 1814, and in 1815 accompanied Louis XVIII to Ghent. Miss Berry (*Letters and Journal*, Vol. III, p. 157) thus describes Madame Marmont, the daughter of the " useful " Perrégaux: " A pretty little woman, but with airs and graces and certain careless impertinence of manner which *réncheried* upon all the *ci-devant* duchesses and marquises." " Marmont himself," she continues, " is rather short, with black hair out of powder, and much beard ; a sensible, intelligent, grave countenance : he put me something in mind of Archbishop Markham's second daughter."

It is a pretty house, one large room and a suite of small ones were open, which were lit up with light of different tints producing some very curious effects. The ornaments, statues, paintings, alabaster vases lamps etc were most beautiful. It was altogether like a fairy palace.

In conversation with an Englishman he told me he had been to the Théâtre Montansier. It was crowded and the spectacle consisted of the most low lived stuff that ever disgraced a stage.

Molière's Farce of M. Pourceaugnac was represented with such additions and embellishments as will not bear recital. This is low and disgusting. The deep moral depravity shewn in what he farther stated furnishes a fearful sample of the effects flowing from infidelity and rash Revolution " I am living " he said " in the Hôtel des Etrangers I dined yesterday with Mr. Stewart who is in the same hotel, and met a large party of Frenchmen chiefly Military and their wives. I asked him how he had made their acquaintance. They are people of fortune he replied and some of the best company in Paris, he had dined at their houses one after another and thought it right to ask them in return. He added that two of the party called upon him this morning and said. Now you are one of our society, come to any of our houses at all times, you will find our wives at home if we are not, make yourself quite at home, dine, and sup whenever you please. We will soon introduce you to our *chère-amies*. Of course you will be aware that with respect to them we are very particular, you will not think of visiting them unless we are ourselves at home."

At the National Library

Jan 19.

Our whole party visited this morning the Bibliothêque Nationale. A very fine collection of books once the Royal Library. On the first floor five large rooms contain 300000 volumes. In one of these rooms is a great piece of rock-work composed I believe of Bronze d'or. It is surmounted by a Pegasus and many allegorical figures. On different parts of it are placed little statues of the French Poets. It is called Le Parnasse Français. In another apartment are two globes, which are 16 or 18 feet in diameter. The gallery of M.S.S. formerly Cardinal Mazarin's and a room or two adjoining contain 80000 vols of M.S.S. in various languages. There is a fine cabinet of medals, and a collection of antiquities chiefly Egyptian. I could obtain no catalogues of them. Another apartment is occupied by a collection of prints arranged in 5000 Portfolios. I asked for one mentioned by Gilpin, a head of our Saviour beautifully engraved in one spiral line, which begins at the tip of the nose and it was produced in a minute. This establishment is open to the public several days in every Decade.

Conseil *d'Etat.*

Paris, le 29 nivôse an 10 de la République.

Thibaudeau Conseiller D'État
à Monsieur Jackson Ministre plénipotentiaire
D'angleterre.

Monsieur

Le C⁰ⁿ Deloche Notaire et M. de Beyer se disposant
à partir après demain pour Londres désirent avoir
votre visa sur leur passeports afin de n'être pas —
inquiétés de Douvres à Londres ; je vous prie de
vouloir bien de leur accorder.

J'ay l'honneur de vous saluer
A. C. Thibaudeau

DEMAND ADDRESSED TO MR. JACKSON BY M. THIBAUDEAU FOR A *VISA*
ON A PASSPORT GRANTED TO TWO PERSONS GOING TO
LONDON, DATED 19 JAN., 1802

Many persons were reading and making extracts notwithstanding the severity of the cold.

Francis and Hill went in the evening to the Minister-of-War. I was so ill with the toothache that I could not go. I know not that I lost more than seeing a fine house full of company.

Jan 20.

Toothache all day. Francis, Hill and George went to the Theatre Montansier. By their account I lost nothing. Had I gone I should certainly have lost my time.

A Solemn Anniversary

Jan. 21

The anniversary of the Death of Louis XVI. In the first years of the Republic this was made the subject of a National Fête. The constituted authorities marched in great pomp to the Champ de Mars, made speeches, and took oaths of hatred to Royalty. This is discontinued. On the anniversary two years ago a black flag was found near the Church of the Madeleine with this inscription "Victimes de la Revolution, venez deposer içi vos vengeances." In the middle a Fleur-de-lys with the words "Vive Louis XVIII." It was perhaps a trick to draw together and catch a few Royalists. [The mind of the young attaché did not, apparently, dwell on these mournful associations, for on the morning of Jan 21 he writes " I was despatched on a shopping expedition with her ladyship of Impey, who had been good enough to take pity on our ignorance, and to offer us the aid of her judgment, in the purchase of lace, as well as to explain for my brother a defect in the Duchess of York's satin shoes, which H.R.H. had commissioned him to get made for her in Paris." This expedition was followed by a visit to the Gobelins tapestry works.[1]]

Francis dined with the Minister-of-Justice, Abrial.[2] There was something odd in his fixing upon such a day, but of course there was no meaning in it.

Jan 22.

Confined to my room with a raging toothache. Francis and Hill went to Madame Récamier, the most beautiful woman in the world and the wife of a rich banker.[3] A party of 200.

Jan. 23

A heavy day. A party of stupid Englishmen dined here.

Divine Service at the Hôtel Caraman

Jan. 24.

Sunday. I officiated to two besides our own

[1] *Diaries and Letters*, p. 52.

[2] Abrial (André Joseph), Count, b. at Annonay (Ardèche) 19 March, 1750, d. at Paris 14 Nov., 1828. Was entrusted with the organization of the Parthenopian Republic in 1800, and subsequently became Minister of Justice, Senator and Peer of France. In 1801–2 he was residing in the Rue Neuve des Petits Champs, which ran from the Rue des Capucines to the Place des Victoires.   [3] See p. 149.

family. Had a congregation of 40 or 50 assembled it would have given me great satisfaction, and have borne a respectable appearance in the eyes of the infidels here. The attempt however has been made, and Francis has given it every support and countenance in his power.

Francis dined with Madame de Stael. She told him a curious story and I beg to know what may be your opinion of it.

" General Oudinot[1] dined with me the other day " said Madame de S. " just after he had killed a man. He told me the whole history of it. He was the evening before in a coffee-house and heard three men abusing in general terms the officers of the Army. Oudinot cautioned them not to speak so freely for he should be obliged to notice it. They disregarded the admonition and continued the abuse. Oudinot challenged them. They immediately accepted this and appointed the place of meeting, desiring him to bring two friends with him. No said Oudinot I shall not take that trouble I shall

---

[1] Oudinot was born in 1767. He early aspired after military renown, obtained a commission, and by his valour and skill rose to be a General of Division. When Bonaparte assumed the Imperial Crown, Oudinot was made a Count of the Empire and Duke of Reggio, and in 1809 a Marshal. He was severely wounded in the Russian Expedition, but preserved his military reputation till he was defeated by Bernadotte and superseded by Marshal Ney. On the abdication of the Emperor he offered his services to Louis XVIII and was made Colonel-General of Grenadiers as well as Military Governor of Metz. In 1823 he served in the invasion of Spain under the Duke d'Angoulême.—D. W.

fight you all three. The next morning they met. M. Choiseul who had been the least forward the day before in the aggression was the bravest in the field and took the first turn. The ball from Oudinot's pistol passed through his head and stretched him lifeless. The other two gentlemen declined encountering the same risk, and so the affair ended. General Oudinot came and dined with me and told me of it."—I suppose no notice will ever be taken of this affair. This General is a very fierce fellow and has several times distinguished himself in these encounters.

Amongst the Studios

Jan. 26th

I went this morning with Francis, Hill, and Lord Aberdeen to see the artists of most distinguished note. First to Vincent.[1] Of the few things he shewed us I could only admire one fine portrait, that of a poet. There was a large sketch of one of the Egyptian Battles, in which appeared a fine even rank of French Grenadiers and Bonaparte alongside of them occupying one half of the canvass and a confused group of Turks on the other side. There was another painting of his in which he represents William

[1] François André Vincent [1746–1816]. A distinguished pupil of Vien and the son of a successful Swiss miniature painter. He won the Grand Prix in 1768 and became a Professor of the Academy in 1792. One of his principal works, " The Battle of the Pyramids," is to be seen at Versailles.

Tell as sinking a boat containing 20 of his enemies.
The painter makes his effect this by placing him
upright on one leg upon a rock while he stretches
out the other to a boat which ought in common
sense to be at some distance from it, presses its
head under water while the crew are tumbling
from it in all directions. This conceited man
gave us a dissertation on the immense superiority
of the French over the rest of the world from
which we were all glad to escape.

We then went to a statuary a sensible and
modest man near 90. David was his *elève*. After
a few minutes very amusing conversation in
which we were all struck with his eloquence and
the flow of his spirits, he led us to his working
room. A noble head of St. Jerome at his devotions
attracted my admiration and seemed to me
perfect if two little cherubims in the corner
were obliterated. He shewed us after many
other things a series of thirty drawings he had
just finished, on the rise and progress of Love.
The frontispiece announced that the artist commenced them at the age of 83. Each drawing
contained from 15 to 20 figures, who told their
story in a remarkably clear and simple manner.
A party of young girls at work. A party at play.
They find a little Cupid asleep. They wake him.
They play with him and nurse him. He slily
wounds one of them ; and so the tale goes on
exhibiting courtship, marriage, an infant, educa-

P

from a back door of the auberge. They are laid out in a magnificent but uninteresting manner. Wide straight walks between thick plantations leading from one large bason of water to another compose the greater part of these stately premises. In these basins Gods, Goddesses and other illustrious personages are placed in various attitudes to serve as spouts to water-works. Many statues and urns of beautiful workmanship are distributed in various parts, and especially before the principal building. We walked through them under the guidance of a waiter from the auberge to the Petit Trianon. This very pretty place, which a few years since was the seat of the most refined elegance and luxury is now occupied by an alehouse keeper who lets out the rooms in summer for the accommodation of parties and furnishes them with refreshments. As we needed not the latter, twenty sous were demanded from each of us. The walls are left bare. Everything that could be destroyed or removed was demolished or carried away by the savages of the Revolution. The garden was laid very prettily, they call it *à l'Anglais*, it consisted of walks winding among thick shrubbery displaying at intervals views of the Château of a sheet of water or of the surrounding country. In one part we ascended a steep eminence, in another were compelled to step cautiously into a dark and cool grotto, where Marie Antoinette would often sit and listen to the stream which bubbled at her and sigh for happiness which Royalty could not give, and ruminate probably on the instability of human greatness. It was a favourite amusement of this unhappy queen to dress herself in a style of rustic simplicity, and inhabit a small cottage from which was excluded every appearance of Royal Pomp. Louis XVI often complied with her taste. He would disguise himself as a farmer and with the Dauphin in the character of a ploughboy visit her in these scenes of innocent enjoyment. The cottage which was litterally a cottage and had nothing in it to raise it above that character either in style or ornament, stands on the banks of a small but beautiful lake. Several other buildings of a similar description are seen half concealed by the surrounding wood. These were destined for the accommodation of the chosen few who were admitted to this private retreat of the royal party. The buildings are now hastening rapidly to decay. They have in some respects suffered by violence. They present altogether a subject for melancholy contemplation. But we had little time for indulging it, and hastened from these to the Grand Trinon, a maison de plaisance on a scale more according with the grandeur of the French monarchy. Noble colonnades of the finest marble excited our admiration, while the grass bursting forth from the crevices of the now

uneven pavement called for our regret. We
could indulge neither more than a few moments
and proceeded to the Château.

This palace stands on a considerable eminence,
and the declivity from the principal front is cut
into large terraces and formal slopes, which
possess a sort of imposing stateliness but no
beauty. We turned to the left to see the Baths
of Apollo, a fine piece of artificial rock work
representing the entrance to the Palace of Thetis.
Thetis is seen in the company of Apollo, and surrounded by her nymphs. The horses of the Sun
are seen in another part attended by Tritons.
A fine basin of water prevents the approach
to these statues ; and a rich wood forms a fine
background to the whole. On entering the Château
we had more reason than ever to regret the being
so limited in time. We were compelled to walk
hastily through rooms hung with fine paintings
and decorated with beautiful sculpture. Great
part of the Palace is converted into Barracks
for a Corps of Invalides, but enough is still shewn
to give the highest ideas of its former magnificence.
After hastening through many spacious apartments and noble galleries we were conducted
to the chapel. This is very superbly decorated,
perhaps too much so. For such decorations are
more calculated to flatter the vanity of the
royal worshipper, than to promote the glory of
that Great Being to whose service it was dedi-

cated, and who requires to be worshipped in spirit and in truth. The richest gilding and ornament were lavished with unsparing hand, and consistently enough you will say, upon the theatre. The architect had so contrived this that it was easily converted into an immense assembly room. When this noble apartment was filled with the highest rank fashion and elegance in France and lighted as it always was on great occasions with 15000 wax candles, the blaze of splendour must have been wonderful. How changed! It is now, and has for several years been dull dark and deserted.

> "Yet Time has seen, that lifts the low
> And level lays the lofty brow,
> Has seen this broken Pile complete,
> Big with the Vanity of State.
> How transient."

We returned from our excursion in time to dine with Lord Mount-Cashel. In the evening Francis and Hill went to Madame Semonville and I home tortured with toothache.

Jan. 27

Toothache accompanied by a swelled face of most frightful distortion, broke up all my plans and made me sigh for home. I hired a carriage.

Jan. 28

Miserably ill but relieved by the thoughts of home. Gilliess dined here.

Jan. 29

Set out early from Paris accompanied by George Jackson[1] and a son of Sir Elijah Impey. We reached Amiens at 11 o'clock at night. Shaw the King's messenger had left that place half an hour before our arrival we proceeded immediately in hopes of overtaking him that we might cross in the same packet. Finding that he gained on us I mounted post horses and reached Boulogne just after he quitted it. Not choosing to go farther in the dark I dispatched a courier with a note to overtake him, and sat down to a very

Once more amongst the Poissardes

comfortable tea-drinking with the aubergist and his family. His wife was a most agreable woman, made many enquiries about England, and answered with great readiness mine respecting her neighbourhood. She described the sufferings of the poor during such a severe winter as the present in a very affecting manner, and spoke of the inability and unwillingness of others to help them as much greater since the Revolution. So I could not help drawing comparisons in favour of my own happy country. Her daughter a lively pretty girl whom I suspected to be the damsel that, sung the song and presented the

[1] George Jackson must have returned to Paris from Amiens, or some other place on the road, as he continued his own diary up to the date of his brother and himself quitting Paris two months later.

bouquet to Francis, told me the English ought
not to have sent such a cross old man as Lord
Cornwallis for when he passed through the town
he received the bouquet in a very cold ungracious
manner. I asked if Monsieur Jackson had not
been favoured with a similar compliment. " O
yes, but he was a young man and much more agreable "—" Then he accepted it in such a way as
to please the giver." " Oh oui, il l'embrassa et
elle etoit fort contente."

Home once more

We overtook the Messenger slept at Calais,
sailed from thence the following morning at
eight, and were landed in five hours at Dover.
I slept there one night and hastened home.

Thirty Years Later

I have thus copied out in a neat form the rough
and hasty sketches which I forwarded to my dear
wife of what I saw and heard when I went to
visit Paris. And I illustrate this copy with
several prints, some of which I purchased there,
some I have recently collected and some still
more valued have been given to me by kind
friends. My object in the trouble I have taken
has been partly to gratify myself in retracing
scenes long gone by ; and which were interesting
in their day ; and partly to give information and
amusement to others. Above all, I wished to

leave a memorial of a remarkable passage in my life to my dear children. I have now only one fear concerning it. The foregoing pages contain mistakes; and I would by no means have any persons who may hereafter read it, draw therefrom any erroneous views, or justify any unchristian practice. In making this transcript I have been led to several serious reflections. I find that in some respects it expresses rather what I thought at the time than what I think now. In my progress through these letters I discovered that with my present views of Christian obligation I should not have left my domestic and parochial Duties for such a journey. I satisfied myself at the time with the leave of my Diocesan and I reposed full confidence in those I left behind to supply my place, but such duties were not confided to me to be so transferred, and I therefore now feel and acknowledge that I was wrong in thus going to France.

But some will not coincide with me in this judgment. They will consider the temptation to have been great, and will think the journey was to be excused, or even to be approved. Should I yield this point; and I have abundant inclination to do so if I could, there yet remains another more difficult to get over. It is a confession I owe to God and to my conscience to acknowledge that I now see a much stronger objection against the spirit in which I went. Had I gone forth into that Land of infidelity and immorality clad in the whole armour of God, an open, faithful, and devoted servant of Christ, bearing testimony by the Word of His Truth against the profligacy round me, it had been something. But alas ! I temporized. I was satisfied with the moral decorums of English good manners, and flattered myself that all was right. For the sake of seeing all I could I went to places of amusement where I ought never to have appeared, and where corruption stalked with unblushing front. I sometimes attended scenes of vanity and folly, and offered no remonstrance against the overwhelming ascendancy of the World, the Flesh and the Devil ; Nay I seemed to compliment it by my presence. My brother-in-law was an amiable and excellent man, in some respects eminently so. We took Bibles and Prayer Books with us, we paid some respect to the Sabbath, we now and then drew comparisons between English religion and French infidelity. And so I bolstered myself up in vanity and self flattery. Christians are not to compare themselves with their fellow sinners, they are not to judge their own conduct by what is done in the world which lyeth in wickedness, they are to judge themselves by the Divine Law. The proper test for human actions is the Word of God. When I resort to that Test, I am immediately led to cry out, " God, be merciful to me a sinner," for I might and ought to have done something in my Heavenly Master's service. I cannot therefore reflect upon my visit to France with unmingled satisfaction.

Yet when I turn my eyes from my own sinfulness and weakness to the goodness and mercy of God, who led me out, and brought me back in safety, who preserved me as far as I could see from the contaminating influence to which I rashly exposed myself, and restored me to the blessings which I had quitted for a while ; when I reflect that I was the first individual permitted by the laws to officiate as a Clergyman in that land where all Religion had been publicly proscribed ; that I had the honour of receiving the first public mark of respect for the sacerdotal order from the existing authorities among a people, by whom ecclesiastics had so recently been put down, plundered, persecuted and murdered, when I think I was thus perhaps the means in the hand of Providence of signifying to the inhabitants of a great city that they might worship God whose existence had been publicly denied, and observe the Sabbath which had been formally abolished, I entertain some hope that my visit to Paris was not fruitless. I feel that a high honour and great mercies were conferred upon me, I desire to acknowledge them with gratitude, and to give glory to God.

APPENDICES

A

GEORGE JACKSON'S JOURNAL

FROM I FEB. TO 20 APRIL, 1802

February 1st.—The First Consul from Lyons on Monday. He entered Paris under a salute of ninety guns, and attended by a brilliant retinue and military escort. The populace assembled in great numbers and welcomed him with loud acclamations. It is rumoured that M. Talleyrand has not been negligent during his absence of the means of strengthening his influence at the Tuileries, and that a marriage between Mademoiselle Archambeau, a niece of M. Talleyrand, and Eugène Beauharnois, Madame B's son, is in contemplation. The consent of the First Consul has not yet been given, and if Fouché resumes his influence probably it will be altogether withheld.

The Italian Republic is the name given to the new country. From the official narrative of the proceedings at Lyons, it would seem that they were conducted with much unanimity, but private letters say they were not ; and the first impression made by the late transactions of the government on those who desire the tranquillity of France and Europe, is that of apprehension. For it is considered that other powers cannot behold with in-difference so considerable an extension of the French Empire, or regard it as a favourable specimen of the First Consul's pacific disposition. " The government of France alone was fully sufficient," they say, " to occupy his time and attention." On the other hand, joy and exultation prevail amongst those men who look only to the gratification of personal ambition and the supremacy of the French nation ; and who think them not too dearly purchased at the expense of private suffering and public calamity.

The " Moniteur " of to-day has a statement, the object of which is to prove that the acquisition of the territory now forming the Italian Republic was indispensably necessary, in order to preserve to France the same proportion of power and influence that she formerly possessed.

4th.—The accounts from Lyons state that the General Assembly made many objections to the constitution imposed on them, and many pertinent remarks on the impropriety of choosing a stranger as the head of it. This produced a considerable disturbance amongst the members, when some officers of the regiments in garrison at Lyons appeared in the hall, and enforced silence on all parties. Bonaparte has sent one of his aides-de-camp— a son of the Third Consul, Le Brun—to Naples with a letter to the king, to thank him for the assistance afforded to some French Troops who were forced by stress of weather to seek refuge in one of the ports of Sicily.

The real aim of this mission, as well as that of General Duroc, who took a letter to the Emperor of Russia, is supposed to be to bring the First Consul into personal correspondence with the sovereigns of Europe by a sort of semi-official means.

Letters—February 6th.—My brother, yesterday, presented several of our countrymen to the First Consul, amongst others Lord Aberdeen,[1] a very agreeable young

---

[1] See *ante*, p. 177.

man, and a great, though a young, friend of Mr. Pitt, who wrote to my brother strongly recommending him, and begging he would show his lordship every attention in his power during his stay in Paris ; consequently, we have seen a good deal of him. Also Mr. Caulfield,[1] a young Irishman just come of age and into a fortune of 30,000*l.* a year, with 100,000*l.* besides, in his pockets to get rid of as fast as he can. As soon as he arrived, he engaged an apartment at an hotel, at ninety louis a month, hired sixteen servants, and has given dinners of thirty covers three times a week, of two louis per head, with innumerable etceteras. Almost any Englishman, Irishman, or Scotchman may drop in if he likes, and be welcome. In the midst of the jovial bachelor's life he is leading, he has received a letter from Lady Crofton—to one of whose daughters he is engaged—that informs him she will be in Paris in a few days with the bride elect and her sisters. The moment, it is thought, is rather ill-chosen ; however, the marriage is to take place in Paris they say.

Lady Crofton's[2] letter was forwarded from London by Mr. Dorant, who was supposed to be at Amiens. But he has thought it advisable, he says, to cross the Channel, and will return in the course of ten days, without his wife even knowing the why and wherefore of his journeys. In the execution of his amateur business as a secret agent

[1] St. George Caulfeild of Donamon Castle, Co. Roscommon He married in 1802 Frances, third daughter of Sir Edward Crofton and Armida his wife. Mr. Caulfeild died in 1812 leaving issue.

[2] Anne, widow of Sir Edward Crofton, second Baronet [1746–1797], m. 1767 Armida, only daughter and heiress of Thomas Croker of Baxtown, Co. Kildare. He died in 1797. In the same year Lady Crofton was raised to the peerage (an honour intended for her late husband) by the title of Baroness Crofton of Mote, Co. Roscommon. Lady Crofton died in 1817.

he will be obliged, he says, to keep such extraordinary company when he arrives, and to do such mysterious things, that he foresees he shall barely escape a lodging in *Le Temple* as the result of his zeal for the interests of England.

Mr. Hill left us on the 2nd, and I have begun, as far as I am able, to supply his place in the confidential department. For, as the business at Amiens is expected to be completed very shortly, no one will be sent out to replace Mr. Hill. This throws, for the time, a good deal of drudgery on my brother—the state of things here obliging him to vie with M. Talleyrand in precaution.

We have had one " Milor " here, who kept a strict incog.—fortunately so, they say—Lord Camelford,[1] who, not being able to obtain a passport, came to Boulogne as an American, and thence in the capacity of a gentleman's servant. He stayed here some time, but fearing that the police might get hold of him he went off to Vienna. It is feared he should attempt some personal mischief.

9th.—The stories of mysterious disappearances, masked midnight visitors, extensive robberies, and other similar events reported in some of the English papers, and which have caused my dear mother so much alarm, are mere inventions. We thought you would have known how little credit such reports are entitled to, and that you hear of us, and from us, often enough to be assured that we are not threatened with any such dangers as you have imagined. It is true that a number of persons have lately been arrested on the plea of a conspiracy against

[1] Thomas Pitt, second Lord Camelford [1775–1804]. He entered the Navy, but was compelled to leave it for gross misconduct. His disorderly conduct in London earned him an unenviable notoriety. He was killed in a duel fought near Holland House.

the life of the First Consul, and that Madame Champenitz,[1] whose husband was governor of the palace on the 10th August, 1792, was yesterday sent for by the police and given into the charge of an officer who had orders not to leave her until she had passed the frontiers of Holland. With this exception, the arrests have been confined to some obscure individuals whose names are said to have been found amongst the papers of the emigrants seized at Bareuth some time since. But these measures are supposed to be taken with the view of intimidating royalists, who have lately been very indiscreet in their conduct.

Last week, some of them were so inconsiderate as to vehemently applaud a play that contained many allusions to the revolution unfavourable to the present order of things. The government instantly ordered the withdrawal of the play.

12th.—We see that the English have also got a story of the written bulletins, and of Bonaparte having reprehended M. de Markoff. The fact is, he treated him as he a short time back treated M. de Lucchesini, and, as those opposed to him say, he is inclined to treat everybody

---

[1] For Champenitz read Champcenetz. The writer evidently refers to the widow of Jean Louis Augustin de Richebourg, Marquis de Champcenetz, who was Governor of the Tuileries during the reign of Louis XVI. In 1789 he resigned his office in favour of his son Louis Pierre, who escaped by a miracle from the horrors of 10 August, 1792, and took refuge in England. His brother was executed on 5 July, 1794. In 1801 the widow of the Governor of the Tuileries resided at No. 576 Rue Saint Florentin. She was the daughter of a rich Dutch merchant, and is frequently mentioned in the memoirs of Madame de Genlis and others. Her exile was ordered, but she, somehow or other, contrived to avoid the consequences of the decree, for in a police report of 9 June, 1803, one reads : " Les Anglais à Fontainebleau se partagent en quatre coteries différentes. . . . Ils ne fréquentent guère les sociétés du pays ; cependant Mme. de Champcenetz en reçoit quelques uns des plus distingués."

Q

who does not profess a wonderful admiration of all he does, and an implicit faith in all he says. As regards the bulletins, it appears there have always been written ones in circulation, professing to give more accurate information on public affairs than can be found in the newspapers.

It might be supposed that the total subjection of the French press would furnish a good chance of success to such an undertaking ; but we are told that these bulletins differ from those of former times only in their conformity to the change of habits, manners, and language ; and that they are still coarse in expression, but less good in intelligence.

However, the author of the present bulletins has been seized, and also his papers. On the list of his subscribers the name of M. de Markoff appeared, and at the last levée Bonaparte asked him whether the information he supplied to his government was derived from the written bulletins.

Everything that is said out of France unfavourable to the wishes or views of this government is always attributed to one or other of the foreign ministers, and I dare say they believe that the observations the English papers indulge in originate with my brother.

14*th*.—When Fouché dined here a few days ago, a reference was made to those reports which have been current of assassinations, &c., with the remark that " with a police so well organized, such a series of depredations as was said to have taken place would be almost impossible." I suppose Fouché considered this was said by way of paying him a compliment, for he answered with that brutal sort of indifference which characterizes him, " Oui, oui, cela va fort bien à présent ; mais pour en venir là il m'a fallu abâttre au moins deux têtes ! "

One can readily believe, after this confession, all the horrors attributed to him at the most furious period of the revolution. I know that it caused a shock to the feelings of more than one person present.

Diaries—Feb. 17th.—The hereditary Prince of Orange[1] dined here last evening—afterwards we went to the Théâtre Français. The prince came about a week ago, for the purpose of ascertaining whether the interests of his family are likely to be benefited, or otherwise, by the peace.

General Duroc,[2] governor of the Tuileries, waited upon him immediately, in the name of the First Consul. The prince has been promised a private audience from day to day, but from day to day M. Talleyrand has made some excuse for deferring it. Meanwhile, the prince is amusing himself with very little dignity, having consented to be introduced by M. de Lucchesini, the Prussian Minister, to a lady of no very high repute, though very high in the favour of M. Talleyrand. M. de L. being aware that the prince was commissioned by the king of Prussia to ask Bonaparte whether he wishes him to be recalled or not—as his wish in either case would be complied with—in order to induce Talleyrand to advise a favourable answer, commenced paying the most servile court to the above-named lady, to whom he promised to introduce the

---

[1] William Frederic, b. 1772, son of William V, b. 1748. On 1 Oct., 1791, the Hereditary Prince of Orange married Frederica Louisa Wilhelmina, daughter of Frederick William II, King of Prussia.

[2] Geraud Christophe Michel Duroc, Duc de Friuli [1772–1813]. Served with great distinction both in the Italian campaign and in Egypt. Returned to France with Bonaparte and was appointed Governor of the Tuileries. Was entrusted with several diplomatic missions, but he did not go to England. Was made a duke in 1808 and a senator in 1813. He was killed at the Battle of Wurtzen, 22 May, 1813, by the same cannon shot which proved fatal to General Kirgener.

prince. The princess, his mother, is most anxious about him, and has written to my brother, who was known to her at the Hague and at Berlin, expressing her fears for her son *sur un pavé si glissant*, and apparently wishing him to see that the prince does not make *un faux pas*. A connection of his family, whom he would scarcely like to meet—the pretended Prince of Nassau—being one of *les intimes* of the lady in question, he has been informed of the circumstance, and for the rest, my brother says, the prince must look to his steps himself.

The marriage that was said to be on the *tapis* is no longer spoken of as at all likely to take place. Bonaparte's success at Lyons has suggested, it is supposed, other and more ambitious schemes, which will be fatal to M. Talleyrand's hopes of strengthening his influence by uniting his niece to the First Consul's stepson.

Madame Bonaparte, a few evenings since, introduced my brother to her daughter,[1] now become her sister-in-law, and has been most amazingly civil to him since he was presented to her. She seems to be so thoroughly good-natured that she might readily be credited with a wish to show attentions, independent of the promptings of her lord and master. But here, nothing is said or done, and least of all in those high quarters, to which some hidden motive is not assigned, and Madame Bonaparte's smiles and words, as they are more or less sunny and gracious, serve some persons as an index of the degree of favour or disfavour, in which they and others are held by the great man himself.

Those of her acquaintance, however, who know her most intimately, assert that her nature is too genial to be regulated after such a fashion—proud as she is of her

[1] Hortense Beauharnais, afterwards Queen of Holland and mother of Napoleon III.

hero—and that, in fact, Bonaparte does not impose such restraints upon her. Many people think her handsome. According to my own private opinion, she is not ; but she is elegant, beautifully dressed, and captivates by her pleasant, good-humoured manner. A Frenchman, who knew her before her second marriage, spoke of her to some Englishmen, who were much pleased with her reception of them, as " une excellente femme, qui a plus de cœur que d'esprit ; d'une tournure agréable, si vous voulez, mais dont la charme infinie de sa grace d'autrefois est effacée par l'air de dignité qu'elle affecte aujourd'hui."

Madame Louis has something of her Mother's manner ; my brother says she has less *bonhomie* in her disposition ; but it may be that youth and better education restrain the free expression of it. It is generally thought that very little, if any, affection exists between her and her husband.

18th.—M. Talleyrand is now occupied with his own marriage,[1] which awaits the arrival of the Pope's dispensation. Meanwhile, he is amassing wealth by making the Department of the Emigrants, which is under his control, as foreign minister, a source of considerable private emolument. He grants, very liberally, permissions to return to France, to those emigrants who can find means to pay him liberally ; whilst Fouché and his police are active in searching out reasons for arresting

[1] The negotiations for Talleyrand's marriage began in February, 1802, through Cardinal Caprara. The first " brief " is dated 10 March, 1802, but it was not " tabled " by the Council of State until 29 June following. The civil marriage was not celebrated until 10 Sept., 1802. The nuptial contract was read on the previous day in the presence of a few friends at Neuilly. It is asserted that a religious ceremony was performed either at Épinay or in the Church of the Foreign Missions in the Rue du Bac, near the Hôtel Gallifet. See *ante*, p. 155, and de Lacombe's *Talleyrand the Man*, pp. 173–83.

a great number of these unfortunate persons when they arrive.

The enmity that exists between these two ministers is occasioned no less by the opposition of their personal characters than by the difference in their public views.

Talleyrand is considered the head of the aristocratic party, Fouché that of the Jacobinical. Talleyrand has something of severity in his manners, and from former habits is disposed to whatever partakes of refinement, even in his vices. Fouché, on the contrary, is as vulgar in deportment, as coarse-minded, and ferocious in disposition. He is, more or less, connected with every species of malefactor, and gratifies his thirst of power and riches by the favouring of one party to the prejudice of another.

20th.—How long, some people ask, can a government, circumstanced as this is, be expected to last ? Others answer, that the great energy and activity of Bonaparte's mind form an almost invincible barrier to the attacks of those who would overthrow him. He secludes himself, now, almost entirely from the public, lives in the Tuileries as in a fortified castle—every possible avenue to it being doubly guarded—and in the midst of a chosen body of veteran troops, already much attached to him, and with whom he employs every means to ingratiate himself still further.

From the frequent change in the commanders of the Consular Guard, it would seem to be Bonaparte's policy not to leave the same officers amongst them long enough to have the opportunity of gaining much influence with the men ; whilst the officers he does appoint are, of course, those he considers most firmly attached to his interests.

General Lannes,[1] who commanded the Consular Guard, and, like Masséna,[2] was much dissatisfied at the prospect of a peace, was suspected of tampering with the men for the purpose of ascertaining how far they would offer opposition in any attempt at revolt. He was dismissed from his command, put under arrest, and afterwards ordered to reside in the country at a fixed distance from Paris. But he has since given up the names of his friends, made known the circumstances of their plot, and accepted the embassy to Portugal, which he at first rejected.

The Abbé Sieyès[3] was also at the head of a set that had combined to oppose Bonaparte's Government. He was offered a national domain of considerable value, which he accepted, and received also the appointment of member of the Sénat conservatim, thus, crushing himself ; for as soon as it was said that his object was pecuniary recompense he fell into contempt, even amongst his warmest adherents, and has been deprived of the power of employing with effect that genius for intrigue for which he is so eminent. Nevertheless, his house is still the resort of all who are disaffected towards the government ; he is easy of access, and gives liberal encouragement to all who think themselves entitled to complain.

[1] Jean Lannes, Duc de Montebello [1769–1809], killed at the Battle of Essling. His title was derived from the place where he fought so bravely on 12 June, 1800.

[2] André Masséna, Duc de Rivoli and Prince of Essling [1758–1817]. His valour and skill contributed very largely to the victory of Marengo. He remained faithful to the Bourbons during the Hundred Days. He has been described as " the first, ablest, and most successful " of the Marshals of the Empire.

[3] Emmanuel Joseph Sieyès [1748–1836]. Helped Bonaparte in the *coup d'état* of 18 Brumaire. Was named Second Consul in 1799, but almost immediately retired from public life. He afterwards accepted the title of Count, but did not return to Paris until after the Revolution of 1830.

But, notwithstanding all the means that are employed to annihilate Bonaparte and his government, those most competent to give an opinion affirm that he can only be overpowered by a much larger, and far more united, force than is, at present, likely to be brought against him ; or by a far more general change of sentiment throughout the country than has hitherto taken place.

Letters—Feb. 25th.—My brother had a very kind hint the other day from Mr. Abbot, as soon as he knew of his intended election and Mr. Wickham's appointment to Ireland,[1] by which the Berlin mission becomes vacant. Although he has a powerful competitor in Mr. Frere,[2] there is a very good chance of my brother gaining the day, as he has learned from trustworthy authority. At all events, he thinks you may rely on his not crossing the Atlantic, for should Mr. F. get Berlin, he will then most probably return to Madrid, for which post Mr. Frere is destined. He would prefer that, he says, to America, though with only the rank of envoy, as it must be put, at least, on an equal footing in point of emolument, and, besides, would not be so much out of the way. He expects to hear soon from Mr. Addington that it is settled provisionally. Vienna will shortly be vacant ; Mr. Paget, who has been there but six months, being, we hear, quite tired of his residence in that capital.

There has been so much writing, that without further assistance it could not be got through ; Mr. Wild, a nephew of Sir Isaac Heard,[3] has therefore joined my brother, and will remain until the end. People are

---

[1] See *ante*, p. xliii.

[2] John Hookham Frere [1769–1846]. Envoy at Lisbon, 1800–2 ; Envoy at Madrid, 1802–4. Distinguished in literature as well as in diplomacy. He retired in 1818 to Malta, where he died.

[3] Sir Isaac Heard [1730–1822], Garter King-at-Arms.

beginning to think that the end has been waited for long enough, and it is said that the delay is on the English side. But it has been announced that Lord Whitworth is ready to set out, and awaits only the signing of the Treaty.

Mr. Dorant has got himself into a scrape. He writes that he had embarked in the Dover packet on his return to Paris, having in his possession five hundred and sixty-nine guineas, but no order for their exportation. By some means it became known at the inn he had slept at, and information of the circumstance was given by the landlord to the Custom-House officer. When Dorant went on board he was seized and searched; the money taken from him, and he was compelled to return on shore. He had a passport from M. Otto, who had given into his charge a parcel, which Dorant describes, in his odd way, as " about three feet long and as thick as a man's thigh, and containing several pieces of flannel for M. Talleyrand." Also he had a lace dress for Madame Bonaparte, for which he had paid sixty guineas; two others for Mesdames Fouché and Luxembourg, as well as green tea and cotton stockings for the latter lady, with two or three patent lace cloaks, and other articles for less distinguished personages. These he was compelled to leave on board, but they were all addressed to the English minister, and were to be passed through the Customs as his. He had the folly to declare that the guineas, as well as the packages, were for the use of the British minister. However, his story was not credited. He excused himself to my brother by saying that it was really a fact, as they enabled him to take a journey in his service, and to be useful to him.

On returning to London he applied to the Foreign Office for the restoration of his money. But Mr. Stone, the Dover agent, had already reported the matter, with, as Dorant says, " the most unfounded and exaggerated insinuations that ever entered into the mind of man to make," and that brought on him, from my Lord Hawkesbury, through Mr. Hammond,[1] reproaches that were most painful to bear. He asked for his money, not that he valued it more than if it had been a bottle of wine, for he was not fond of money, and had already more than he should live to spend ; but it was the way of losing it that hurt him so deeply. My lord could not understand why he should go to France in such a manner, nor what secret there was between him and His Majesty's minister, when he gave them information which, they said, changed completely the face of the thing, and Mr. H., who had declared that he had never known of an instance of money once seized being restored, then promised him some compensation. This he declined ; he would have the whole or none. He is likely it appears to get none, for he had heard nothing more on the subject, and has not made any further application, being well satisfied, he says, if they will leave him alone. He declares that he had information that would have enabled Lord Cornwallis to have the Treaty signed on his own terms within forty-eight hours.

For the present, I suppose, he has given up his self-imposed duty of collecting secret intelligence, for he knows not, he says, when he may be able to revisit Paris. This is a disappointment and loss to others, no less than to himself ; he has such a talent for worming out secrets, and does it so thoroughly *con amore*. I believe he has found it also not an unprofitable pastime, even should he

[1] George Hammond [1763–1853], Merton College, Oxford. M.A. and Fellow, 1787. Entered the Diplomatic Service in 1788. Was Under-Secretary for Foreign Affairs, 1795–1806. Joint-Editor of the *Anti-Jacobin*.

eventually not recover in some form the value of the guineas seized at Dover.

March 2nd.—What a dismal set of table-talkers you have at Bath, my dear mother, with their stories of the king's want of strength, and Mr. Addington's want of strength ; themselves, I think, deficient in that sort of strength they think the king wanting in ; for my brother had yesterday a letter from Mr. Harcourt, dated Windsor Lodge, in which he says all the family is quite well. You have levées and drawing-rooms as usual ; and as Mrs. Lawrell, we hear, adds so much to the warmth of the latter, their Majesties must be in good health to support the fatigue of them.

It is not in the papers, but that is not very conclusive, that the Duke of York has recently lost 200,000*l.*, and is selling his town house and horses.[1] At all events you have the Duchess amongst you, though, as you suggest, only to be out of the way, he having brought her down and returned to town the next day. We have a Bath letter of later date than yours, which says that the Duchess has been bitten in the hand by one of her dogs ; that the wound will not heal, and that her physician has recommended her to try the Bath waters.—Oh, the wonder-working waters !—Her royal highness, we are told, " has her hand pumped upon, and then takes one glass of water after everybody has left the little pump-room, as she would avoid as much as possible being seen." I hope you will not fail to inform us of the happy result, and my brother says you are to lay him at her royal highness's *feet*, and inquire if she wants any more shows before he leaves Paris.

Diaries—March 4th.—Bonaparte is furious at what is

---

[1] Mr. Dawson Warren had been appointed Chaplain to the Duke of York in 1796.

said of him in our papers. Pelletier's[1] journal has been complained of. M. Talleyrand has mentioned with much dissatisfaction the hostile feeling which, as he asserts, the English ministerial newspapers display towards France. " Ce n'est pas là la manière d'agir," he said, " mais, malgré tout cela, nous ferons la paix." . He added, however, a sort of threat, if those unscrupulous attacks were not discontinued, to " Lâcher " his papers against us, which would produce, he said, a by no means pleasant sort of warfare.

Both the " Times " and the " Morning Chronicle " have copies of articles respecting my brother, from Montliver's " Journal de Londres," a paper in the pay of this government. All its articles on the public and private affairs of France are supplied from the Tuileries and Fouché's office, and there is a person here, connected with the " Morning Chronicle," whose business is to explain what his colleague dares not bring forward in his semi-official shape. Hence the indecent paragraphs in the " Chronicle " respecting persons high and low in this country. The story of the king's intention to abdicate has produced a most unpleasant effect on the Continent, where there are no means of knowing the falsehood of such like reports.

10th.—We are to have Mrs. Damer[2] and her friend, Miss Berry, here in a few days. Two such connoisseurs in every way, would not, of course, lose the first oppor-

---

[1] Pelletier was tried in London for the libels on Bonaparte and convicted, but never sentenced. The rupture of May, 1803, put an end to the proceedings. Pelletier subsequently failed to obtain the recognition of his services he hoped for from Louis XVIII.

[2] Anne Seymour Damer [1749–1828], m. John Damer of Milton Abbey, Dorset, 1767. Was famous as a sculptress, and presented Napoleon with a bust of Fox. She accompanied Miss Berry to Paris in 1802, and for some time corresponded with the Empress Josephine.

tunity of visiting Paris to see the Apollo Belvidere and other fine sights. Lord Pelham[1] would not give them a passport till now, and he does not say what made him change his determination. They will see pictures and statues enough to satisfy them, I hope.

M. David, the painter of the fine picture of the passage of Mont St. Bernard, has completed one of the Roman and Sabine warriors ; the Sabine woman interposing to prevent the fight. The artist has published an apology for the nakedness of these bold warriors. Mont St. Bernard, with Bonaparte and his heroes, pleases me better than this scuffle of naked savages and wild women —so much for my taste. What would Miss Berry say, I wonder ?

Sir Ralph Woodford's son has just arrived here from Egypt, where he has been with Major Byng, who was reported dead after the battle of Hohenlinden. Mr. Windham[2] wrote to my brother about the major, who is his nephew, and took the opportunity of giving him a strong dash of his politics. To-morrow we all go to St. Germain, a few miles from Paris, to see " Esthère," one of Racine's plays acted by the young ladies of a famous boarding-school kept by a Madame Campan. She was a bed-chamber woman of the poor Queen Marie Antoinette, and has, by her cleverness and character, been able to keep up her school during the whole of the revolution upon the same footing.

12th.—The strange intelligence with which Dorant was primed, when so inopportunely stopped on his voyage to France, he has found a way of conveying to my brother, and Lord Cornwallis has received some hints, of which

---

[1] Thomas Pelham, second Earl of Chichester [1756–1826]. Educated at Westminster and Cambridge. Was Home Secretary under Addington, 1801–3.

[2] William Windham, see *ante*, p. 25.

it is supposed he might make some advantageous use. But hints, it is thought, are not readily taken in that quarter. There has been much delay for some days in the transmission of the reports of the proceedings at Amiens. Perhaps it would be almost high treason to say that the discussions are protracted unnecessarily by the English Negotiator ; but the very *merry* letters that find their way hither from the seat of Congress give such amusing details of the " pottering old woman's " leisurely mode of transacting business, that one cannot refrain from hearty laughter *sous cape*, while the object of it is, of course, cried up as a sort of British Solomon. He is, indeed, looked upon as a fine old boy, and as conscientiously desirous to do the work he has been charged with, in the best manner. But, as if aware that he is not qualified for it, he cannot move a step without reference to England. This, my brother says, is much to be regretted, as it affords the French Government a pretext, they are only too glad to avail themselves of, for their complaints against England.

15*th*.—Public attention is wholly absorbed by the delay in the signing of the Definitive Treaty. It is commented upon in every society, and, in some instances, with expressions so disrespectful towards the English Government that it has been found necessary to take notice of them. Serious doubts prevail as to the final issue of the Congress, and it is suspected that the idea of a rupture of the negotiation is now floating in the mind of Bonaparte. In the official " Moniteur " it is unequivocally asserted that the signature is retarded solely by His Majesty's Government. This statement ends with an appeal to the British nation, by which the First Consul, who is himself the author of it, seems to wish by anticipation to throw off the odium which a renewal of the war might bring upon him. It is made to appear, also, that the principal powers of Europe concur in his plans and operations. Yet it is believed that, owing to the internal state of the country, and the situation of the armament of St. Domingo, the First Consul, himself, will not desire to renew the war ; but that from the jumble of interests that exists here, and which must be taken into consideration, he experiences as much difficulty from the approach of peace as he ever met with in the conduct of the war. Difficulties press upon him, and they are of a nature which his temper and frame of mind are ill-suited to overcome, and seem to put him off his guard against the danger that menaces him.

War, then, may serve his object better than peace, as it would enable him to employ many of his bitterest enemies in distant situations, where their thirst of military glory and military plunder would be gratified, which for a time would stifle all feeling of resentment against him.

18th.—A whole batch of presentations awaits the signing of the Treaty. Mrs. Damer and Miss Berry, who arrived the other day, will be of the number.[1] *En*

---

[1] In the Berry *Letters and Diaries*, Vol. II, pp. 122–92, Miss Berry makes several allusions to meeting Mr. Francis James Jackson at dinners and other social functions, most of which are not referred to in the index of the book. She left Paris on 11 April. On 1 April she had been presented to Bonaparte's mother, and on 8 April to his wife. On the latter occasion she and Mrs. Damer had a very interesting conversation with the First Consul, who praised the fine voice of Mrs. Billington. On 2 June following Anne Damer wrote to Sir Joseph Banks :—

" I transmit you a note which I have received from Madame Bonaparte, and which most particularly concerns you—it is, I think, uncommonly polite and obliging, and I doubt not but you will, as far as you can, comply with her request. I believe I mentioned to you my having taken the liberty of joining your name with mine in the *envoy* of seeds, etc., which I made, as, of course, setting apart the particular value I well knew it would *attendant* they are fully employed, and highly delighted with the spoils of war with which this gay city is enriched. The weather is become so mild and fine that we can now go the round of the sights again with some pleasure. It is high spring in the garden of this house, flowers are peeping forth, and the ground is so well laid out that, if the Treaty should remain much longer unsigned, and war not be the consequence, I foresee, that we shall have some pleasant al fresco entertainments. The last two mild evenings our foreign visitors took their coffee in the garden and smoked there.

19th.—Some connoisseurs, who had been inspecting the pictures, condemned much the retouching by French artists, which some of the finest works of the old Italian masters have undergone since their arrival. They ought, they contended, to have been exhibited in the condition in which they were received. But it appears they were so much injured in their transport, that some of the most valuable paintings could not have been shown without the restoration of the defaced portions. But the wreck of the original works, connoisseurs say, would have given all true lovers of art more pleasure than the renovations and botchings, as they are termed, of incompetent artists. However, the most skilful painters have been employed on them, and time will efface the traces of the modern brush.

20th.—M. Talleyrand had a long conversation with my brother yesterday on the " inexplicable conduct of the English Government." All the principal articles of the Treaty having been agreed to, eight or ten days ago, he finds it difficult to understand the delay in signing

give them, it was but proper that she should know from whom in reality the present came. I shall wait to return Madame Bonaparte my thanks for her very flattering expressions, and for employing me in her commissions, till I hear from you."
[MSS. A. M. Broadley

it. Nothing could exceed, he says, the surprise of the First Consul when he learned that Lord Cornwallis had received fresh instructions, which directed him to reject what he had already consented to sign.

Notwithstanding these remonstrances and their profession of anxiety for the conclusion of peace, my brother declares that he can observe in the conduct of the French Government nothing that bears an appearance of the cordiality and good faith so liberally observed by England towards France, but, on the contrary, deep duplicity and an eager desire to take every possible unfair advantage to increase their own power and influence, and to separate England from the rest of the world.

22nd.—It was remarked in conversation yesterday how large a number of Generals of inferior note had latterly been appointed to the Sénat conservatim, and it was explained that it was a means adopted by the First Consul for dissolving, without *éclat*, the military confederacy formed against him, it being, while doing so a great object with him also to impress the world with a belief that his government is carried on without any opposition or extraordinary exertion of authority.

26th.—At last ! A French courier has brought the Treaty. He made the journey with such unusual speed that he reached Paris from Amiens in nine hours and a half ![1]

[1] This would create an impression that the treaty must have been signed on 25 March and not on 27 March—the date of its promulgation (see *post*, p. 259). Under the date 26 March Miss Berry writes in her journal :—

" Dined at Mr. Jackson's (our Minister). He is well lodged in a *rez-de-chaussée* apartment in the Hôtel de Caraman, Rue St. Dominique. The company consisted of Madame Brignole, Madame de Staël, the *ci-devant* Abbé, now M. de St. Phar, the Prince Auguste d'Arenberg, Baron Amfelt, Adrien de Montmorency, the Swedish Minister (Baron Ehrenswerd), the Marquis of Douglas, and General Marmont's wife."—(Vol. II, p. 156.)

R

cause of it, it may be inferred, from some transactions that took place on the *Bourse* a fortnight ago, that it was to afford an opportunity to make good a considerable deficiency in the money matters of some persons connected with the government, in consequence of the Treaty not having been signed, as was expected, ten days sooner. But however this may be, it is certain that as little time as possible was lost between the arrival of the courier and the communication of the Treaty.

31st.—As a sort of prelude to the publication of the *Concordatum*,[1] orders were given on Saturday for a *Te Deum* to be sung, and high mass to be celebrated the next day, by Cardinal Caprera,[2] at the Cathedral of Notre Dame. Notice was sent to the Cardinal to be ready for the ceremony, which was to be conducted with great pomp and magnificence. But early on Sunday morning he was informed that it was not to take place. This change of intention is supposed to be owing to the difficulty of so soon displacing the constitutional clergy, who now have possession of Notre Dame, and to the impossibility of fitly preparing the church, at so short a notice, for so solemn an event as the restoration of divine worship in France. For Notre Dame, like other sacred edifices, was pillaged and defaced at the time of the revolution, and has since fallen, from neglect, into a dirty, ruinous condition.

The public reception of the cardinal as the Pope's legate will take place with the publication of the *Concordatum*.

[1] The Concordat was promulgated on Easter Sunday, 18 April, 1802. Bonaparte and the other Consuls were present at the great national fête which took place in Notre Dame. A State dinner was given at the Tuileries in the evening. See *post*, p. 248.

[2] Giovanni Battista Caprara [1733–1810]. Cardinal Caprara subsequently crowned Napoleon King of Italy. He died in Paris, old, blind, and infirm.

THE TREATY OF AMIENS

AS PORTRAYED IN A CONTEMPORARY SYMBOLICAL PRINT PUBLISHED IN PARIS UNDER THE AUSPICES
OF THE FIRST CONSUL IN THE SPRING OF 1802

Report says that the offices of Second and Third Consul will be abolished about the same time, and that Bonaparte will take exclusively to himself the nominal as well as the real direction of affairs.

The hereditary Prince of Orange speaks in terms of much regret of a title different from that his family has usually borne being now to be adopted by it.

Letters—April 2nd.—We do not yet know when we shall leave Paris, but until we leave we are gentlemen at large, with little to do but to amuse ourselves.[1]

It is strange, that the anxious interest which the people generally seemed to take in the Congress at Amiens, during the early stage of its deliberations, has subsided into utter indifference since the final result was known. The First Consul is greatly mortified at the apathy of the people, and did not conceal his displeasure from the trade deputations, when they presented themselves to congratulate him on the re-establishment of peace.[2]

[1] Mr. Jackson does not chronicle the Sunday dinner of 4 April, when Miss Berry and Mrs. Damer met Madame Récamier at the hospitable table of the British Minister Plenipotentiary.

[2] The First Consul certainly did his best to popularize the Peace. He inspired a very interesting symbolical print which was engraved by Le Beau after the design of Nodet and published by Jean at 32 Rue Jean de Beauvais, whose shop on the south side of the Seine was as popular as that of Martinet in the Rue du Coq, St. Honoré, in the north. It bears the somewhat incorrect title of " The Treaty of Peace signed at Amiens on March 24, 1802." Bonaparte, the pacificator of Europe, is portrayed as assembling the Powers of Europe, who swear to the Peace on the altar of Good Faith, while Peace in person extends a protecting hand to the arts which hasten to her call. The genius of France burns even the relics of victory, while Consular Influence personified by Pallas, holding a rudder and armed with a club, drives away War, Envy, and Discord, who take refuge in the Temple of Janus Bifrons. A maritime port and vessels represent the liberty of the sea, and Fame announces the glorious event to the whole universe.

He received them with great coldness, and gave them clearly to understand that, as he had diligently laboured to secure for the French nation an advantageous peace, he looked for some more decided manifestation of thankfulness, than he had hitherto received, from those who were most to be benefited by his patriotic efforts. The poorer classes still clamour for the cheap bread they are, unfortunately, not likely to get ; and the commercial people who looked for a great revival of trade, as soon as only the preliminaries were ratified, are of course still disappointed. However, all the hotels are overflowing with English ; for we have an inundation from our shores since the signature of the Treaty, and the flood increases daily, and will no doubt go on increasing. The Parisians take every possible advantage of this, treating all our countrymen as " les riches milors." Those who find their way to this house complain loudly ; extortion, they say, is the rule with the shopkeepers in their dealings with their visitors, and on all sides they fleece them most thoroughly.

6th.—Perhaps this will be the last letter I shall send you from Paris, for my brother has received his letter of recall, and waits only for an audience to deliver it. He reckons on setting out in a fortnight. Although established so short a time, there are a great many things to do, and many people to take leave of, before setting off. Nothing is said to him from Downing Street of his future destination ; but he still preserves the hope of not leaving Europe.

8th.—M. Talleyrand informed my brother, on his requesting permission to take leave of the First Consul, that it would be informal, and inconsistent with the rules of etiquette established here, to take leave so abruptly. He reminded him that his orders were to return immediately ; Mr. Merry, who had conducted the business at Amiens, being fixed on by His Majesty's Government as the proper person to exchange Treaties, and succeed him as minister until the arrival of an ambassador. No day is however yet fixed for his audience.

General Berthier,[1] the minister of war, is spoken of as likely to have the London embassy. No doubt he would be glad to accept it, as he is displeased with some retrenchments lately made in his department by the First Consul, and has, besides, *liaisons* which he would be glad, *on dit,* to escape from ; not being able to carry off those affairs with so high a hand as his colleague, M. Talleyrand.

Diaries—April 11*th.*—The *Concordatum* between this government and the Church of Rome, and the different articles by which it provides for a Church Establishment in France, received the sanction of the *corps legisl.* on the 8th. On the following day Cardinal Caprera was admitted to an audience of the First Consul as *legate à latere,* from his Holiness the pope.

It is reported that the ceremony was conducted in a manner in every respect similar to that which was customary under the former government.

12*th.*—The First Consul has finally fixed on Easter Sunday for the festivities in honour of the general peace.

13*th.*—All is bustle, activity, and animation ; and if the peace itself is disregarded, the keenest anxiety is yet shown, by all classes of this *peuple mobile,* to celebrate it with the utmost *éclat.*

16*th.*—As the 18th approaches, Paris becomes fuller,

---

[1] Louis Alexandre Berthier [1755–1814]. Assisted the escape of the aunts of Louis XVI. Chef d'état-major to the army in Italy. Commanded at Rome, 1798. Accompanied Bonaparte to Egypt. In 1799 became War Minister. Created Prince de Neufchâtel, 1806, and later Prince of Wagram. Took part in the Russian Campaign. Accompanied Louis XVIII to Ghent in 1815. Was murdered at Bamberg

and nothing seems to interest any one which has not some reference to the forthcoming fêtes. Many visitors flock in daily from the provinces, where Bonaparte is said to be very popular ; and where, generally, the inhabitants consider themselves indebted to him for the tranquillity of the last two years. They seem to have no particular motive for dissatisfaction with the present order of things —which, if not perfect, they think is as good as any they have yet known—but such as may arise from an un-extinguished sentiment of attachment to their legitimate sovereign, and to the religion of their fathers. These feelings are said to be most prevalent in the south of France ; they are not, however, strong enough to induce any active exertion.

19*th*.—Easter morning was ushered in by some passing showers, but the whole city was in motion very early. Throngs of sight-seers—some not a little bespattered— picked their way through the muddy pools of the Paris streets, avoiding, as best they could, the crazy *fiacres* that dodged about in greater numbers, and caused greater confusion than ever.

The First Consul gave an early audience to the *corps diplomatique* before going in procession to Notre Dame.

The *Concordatum* was published to the sound of trumpets and the thunder of artillery, and the joy of the populace seemed unbounded ; for with many the religious part of the ceremony was the principal attraction. The Pope's legate was, therefore, the object of profound veneration, and fairly divided the honours of the day with the " nation's great benefactor," by whom this happy change, "peace on earth, peace with the Church and with Heaven," has been brought about.

Admission to Notre Dame was by tickets, for all who were not present officially ; yet the cathedral was in every part crowded to excess, so numerous and urgent had the applicants been.

So short a time had been allowed for the decorating and embellishing the interior of the building, that we were the more struck, on entering, with the change from the dirt and desolation of the other day to the pomp and splendour of yesterday.

The *Te Deum* was sung magnificently, and with deep feeling ; many persons found it difficult to restrain their emotion, while not a few were overpowered by it. For this first solemn celebration of high mass necessarily awakened the saddest feelings, and the most painful memories, in the greater part of the congregation.

The carriages of the First Consul and his colleagues, and the green, gold-embroidered liveries of their attendants, were exceedingly rich. Some of the principal officers, and the foreign ministers generally, made a respectable part of the show in that way ; but, although Spartan simplicity is no longer the order of the day, a decent private vehicle is still a rarity, and citizen coachmen are still unliveried.

At the audience of the morning, my brother took leave of the First Consul. In reply to the assurance that it was " His Majesty's desire to cement the union and good understanding now happily re-established between the French Republic and England," he requested that the king might be informed that it was " equally his sincere determination to employ every means in his power to render the peace durable, and productive of mutual satisfaction and advantage."

He then noticed the circumstance of my brother having been the first minister appointed to this country after the cessation of hostilities, and expressed in very obliging terms the recollection which he said he should retain of his having been here, and his wish that his future destination might be in every respect satisfactory to him. Later, my brother made his final bow to Madame ; and to-day he takes leave of the Second and Third Consuls and M. Talleyrand.

We had a dinner in celebration of the great events that were fêted yesterday, and afterwards we went to look at the illuminations, in which the French are said to excel.

That of the British mission represented a temple—the closed temple of Janus, I believe—with many columns, round which thousands of coloured lamps were wreathed. It was a very effective display, and was greatly admired.[1]

The streets were thronged with a very orderly mob of sight-seers, and, for the general convenience and safety, no *fiacres* were allowed to be out that evening.

The public buildings, the residences of the members of the government, and those of the foreign ministers, were all brilliantly lighted up. The Place Vendôme, Place de la Revolution, &c., glowed with colour from the many-tinted lamps.

The Palais du Corps Législatif—once the Palais Bourbon—was compared to a palace of jewels, so thickly was it covered with gleaming lamps, and their colours so harmoniously intermixed. The entire length of the Tuileries was marked by lines of fire, and festooned with flowers and variegated lamps, and draped with numerous flags ; those of all nations intermingling with the *drapeau republicain*. A portion of the gardens was illuminated ;

[1] Mr. Jackson seems to have adopted the device from the Bonaparte print. There were also illuminations on a large scale in London, but M. Otto was less fortunate in Portman Square in 1802 than he had been in Hereford Street in 1801. The mob mistook " Concord " for " Conquered," and the general indignation was increased by the absence of a crown over the G. R. At the last moment the word " Concord " was changed to " Amitié."

in the vicinity was a display of fireworks, and another on the river ; while a concert of military bands enlivened the scene.

Outside the grounds, and near the palace, a temporary fountain had been erected. Last evening it streamed with bright Bourdeauz, and many a bumper was quaffed there in honour of " La paix et le pacificateur ! " and in one instance we heard : " Le héros ! qui veut se faire aimer en *vin !—en vain.*"

Whatever the peace itself may prove to be, the brilliant *fête de nuit* with which it has been celebrated was an undoubted success ; and, I am glad we have had the opportunity of witnessing that, as well as the solemn ceremonies of the morning.

20th.—All our arrangements are completed ; and to-morrow morning, early, we shall be *en route* for Old England. We have lived for five months in a perfect maze of plots, Jacobin, military, and royalist ; surrounded by spies, noting every act, and reporting every word ; yet I, at least, leave the gay capital with regret. And gay, indeed, it is, for notwithstanding the undercurrent of stratagem and intrigue, in general society a genial tone lies on the surface, and a lively *sans façon* mode of life prevails that is irresistibly pleasing and attractive.

B

PRELIMINARY ARTICLES OF PEACE BETWEEN HIS BRITANNIC
MAJESTY AND THE FRENCH REPUBLIC, SIGNED AT
LONDON (IN ENGLISH AND FRENCH), THE 1ST OF OCTOBER,
1801 ; THE 9TH VENDEMIAIRE, YEAR 10 OF THE FRENCH
REPUBLIC.

(Published by Authority.)

HIS MAJESTY the King of the United Kingdom of
Great Britain and Ireland, and the First Consul of the
French Republic, in the name of the French People,
being animated with an equal desire of putting an end to
the calamities of a destructive war, and of re-establishing
union and good understanding between the two countries,
have named for this purpose ; namely, his Britannic
Majesty, the Right Hon. Robert Bank Jenkinson, com-
monly called Lord Hawkesbury, one of his Britannic
Majesty's Most Honourable Privy Council, and his
Principal Secretary of State for Foreign Affairs ; and
the First Consul of the French Republic, in the name of
the French People, Citizen Lewis William Otto, Commissary for the Exchange of French Prisoners in England ;
who, after having duly communicated to each other their
full powers, in good form, have agreed on the following
Preliminary Articles :

ART. I. As soon as the Preliminaries shall be signed
and ratified, sincere friendship shall be re-established
between his Britannic Majesty and the French Republic,
by sea and by land, in all parts of the world ; and in
order that all hostilities may cease immediately between
the two Powers, and between them and their Allies
respectively, the necessary instructions shall be sent with
the utmost dispatch to the Commanders of the Sea and

Land forces of the respective States; and each of the Contracting Parties engages to grant passports and every facility requisite to accelerate the arrival, and ensure the execution of these orders. It is further agreed, that all conquests which may have been made by either of the Contracting Parties from the other, or from their respective Allies, subsequently to the Ratification of the present Preliminaries, shall be considered as of no effect, and shall be faithfully comprehended in the restitutions to be made after the Ratification of the Definitive Treaty.

Art. II. His Britannic Majesty shall restore to the French Republic and her Allies, namely, to his Catholic Majesty and to the Batavian Republic, all the possessions and colonies occupied or conquered by the English forces in the course of the present war, with the exception of the island of Trinidad, and the Dutch possessions in the island of Ceylon, of which island and possessions his Britannic Majesty reserves to himself the full and entire sovereignty.

Art. III. The port of the Cape of Good Hope shall be open to the commerce and navigation of the two Contracting Parties, who shall enjoy therein the same advantages.

Art. IV. The island of Malta, with its dependencies, shall be evacuated by the troops of his Britannic Majesty, and restored to the Order of St. John of Jerusalem. For the purpose of rendering this Island completely independent of either of the two Contracting Parties, it shall be placed under the guarantee and protection of a third Power, to be agreed upon in the Definitive Treaty.

Art. V. Egypt shall be restored to the Sublime Porte, whose territories and possessions shall be preserved entire, such as they existed previously to the present war.

Art. VI. The territories and possessions of her Most Faithful Majesty shall likewise be preserved entire.

Art. VII. The French forces shall evacuate the kingdom of Naples and the Roman territory. The English forces shall in like manner evacuate Porto Ferrajo, and, generally, all the ports and islands which they may occupy in the Mediterranean, or in the Adriatic.

Art. VIII. The Republic of the Seven Islands shall be acknowledged by the French Republic.

Art. IX. The evacuations, cessions, and restitutions, stipulated for by the present Preliminary Articles, shall take place in Europe within one month ; in the Continent and Seas of America and Africa, within three months ; and in the Continent and Seas of Asia, within six months, after the Ratification of the Definitive Treaty.

Art. X. The prisoners made respectively shall, immediately after the exchange of the Definitive Treaty, all be restored, and without ransom, on paying reciprocally the debts which they may have individually contracted. Discussions having arisen respecting the payment for the maintenance of prisoners of war, the Contracting Powers reserve this question to be settled by the Definitive Treaty, according to the law of nations, and in conformity to established usage.

Art. XI. In order to prevent all causes of complaint and dispute which may arise on account of prizes which may be made at sea after the signature of the Preliminary Articles, it is reciprocally agreed, that the vessels and effects which may be taken in the British Channel and in the North Seas, after the space of twelve days, to be computed from the exchange of the Ratifications of the present Preliminary Articles, shall be restored on each side ; that the term shall be *one* month from the British Channel and the North Seas, as far as the Canary Islands inclusively, whether in the Ocean, or in the Mediterranean: two months from the said Canary Islands as far as the Equator ; and, lastly, five months in all parts of the world, without any exception, or any more particular description of time or place.

Art. XII. All sequestrations imposed by either of the parties on the funded property, revenues, or debts, of any description, belonging to either of the Contracting Powers, or to their subjects or citizens, shall be taken off immediately after the signature of the Definitive Treaty. The decision of all claims brought forward by individuals of the one country against individuals of the other, for private rights, debts, property, or effects whatsoever, which, according to received usages and the law of nations ought to revive at the period of peace, shall be heard and decided before the competent tribunals ; and in all cases prompt and ample justice shall be administered in the countries where the claims are made. It is agreed, moreover, that this Article, immediately after the Ratification of the Definitive Treaty, shall apply to the Allies of the Contracting Parties, and to the individuals of the respective nations, upon the condition of a just reciprocity.

Art. XIII. With respect to the Fisheries on the coasts of the island of Newfoundland, and of the islands adjacent, and in the Gulph of St. Lawrence, the two Powers have agreed to restore them to the same footing on which they were before the present War, reserving to themselves the power of making, in the Definitive Treaty, such arrangements as shall appear just and reciprocally useful, in order to place the fishing of the two nations on the most proper footing for the maintenance of Peace.

Art. XIV. In all cases of Restitution agreed upon by the present Treaty, the fortifications shall be delivered up in the state in which they may be at the time of the signature of the present Treaty, and all the works which shall have been constructed since the occupation shall remain untouched.

It is further agreed, that in all the cases of cession stipulated in the present Treaty, there shall be allowed to the inhabitants, of whatever condition or nation they may be, a term of three years, to be computed from the notification of the Definitive Treaty of Peace, for the purpose of disposing of their properties, acquired and possessed either before or during the present war ; in the which term of three years they may have the free exercise of their religion and enjoyment of their property.

The same privilege shall be granted in the countries restored, to all those who shall have made therein any establishments whatsoever during the time when those countries were in the possession of Great Britain.

With respect to the other inhabitants of the countries restored or ceded, it is agreed, that none of them shall be prosecuted, disturbed, or molested in their persons or properties, under any pretext, on account of their conduct or political opinions, or of their attachment to either of the two Powers, nor on any other account, except that of debts contracted to individuals, or on account of acts posterior to the Definitive Treaty.

Art. XV. The present Preliminary Articles shall be ratified, and the Ratifications exchanged at London, in the space of fifteen days for all delay ; and immediately after their Ratification, Plenipotentiaries shall be named on each side, who shall repair to Amiens, for the purpose of concluding a Definitive Treaty of Peace in concert with the Allies of the Contracting Parties.

In witness whereof, We the Undersigned, Plenipotentiaries of his Britannic Majesty, and of the First Consul of the French Republic, by virtue of our respective full powers, have signed the present Preliminary Articles, and have caused our seals to be put thereto.

Done at London, the 1st day of October, 1801, the 9th Vendemiaire, Year 10 of the French Republic.

HAWKESBURY.   OTTO.
     (L.S.)   (L.S.)

C

PROCLAMATION

LES CONSULS DE LA RÉPUBLIQUE AUX FRANÇAIS

FRANÇAIS, vous l'avez enfin tout entière cette paix que vous avez méritée par de si longs et de si généreux efforts.

Le monde ne vous offre plus que des nations amies, et sur toutes les mers s'ouvrent pour vos vaisseaux des ports hospitaliers.

Fidèle à vos vœux et à ses promesses, le gouvernement n'a cédé ni à l'ambition des conquêtes ni à l'attrait des entreprises hardies et extraordinaires. Son devoir était de rendre le repos à l'humanité et de rapprocher par des liens solides et durables cette grande famille européenne dont la destinée est de faire la destinée de l'univers.

Sa première tâche est remplie, une autre commence pour tous et pour lui. A la gloire des combats, faisons succéder une gloire plus douce pour les citoyens, moins redoutable pour nos voisins.

Perfectionnons, mais surtout apprenons aux générations naissantes à chérir nos institutions et nos lois. Qu'elles croissent pour l'égalité civile, pour la liberté publique, pour la prospérité nationale. Portons dans les ateliers de l'agriculture et des arts cette ardeur, cette constance, cette patience qui ont étonné l'Europe dans toutes nos circonstances difficiles. Unissons au efforts

s

du gouvernement les efforts des citoyens pour enrichir, pour féconder toutes les parties de notre vaste territoire.

Soyons le lien et l'exemple des peuples qui nous environnent. Que l'étranger qu'un intérêt de curiosité attirera parmi nous s'y arrête, attaché par le charme de nos mœurs, par le spectacle de notre union, de notre industrie et par l'attrait de nos jouissances, qu'il s'en retourne dans sa patrie plus ami du nom français, plus instruit et meilleur.

S'il reste encore des hommes que tourmente le besoin de hair leurs concitoyens ou qu'aigrisse le souvenir de leurs pertes, d'immenses contrées les attendent : qu'ils osent aller y chercher des richesses et l'oubli de leurs infortunes. Les regards de la patrie les y suivront, elle secondera leur courage ; un jour, heureux de leurs travaux, ils reviendront dans son sein, dignes d'être citoyens d'un état libre et corrigés du délire des persécutions.

Français, il y a deux ans, ce même jour vit se terminer vos dissensions, s'anéantir toutes les factions. Dès lors vous pûtes concentrer toute votre énergie, embrasser tout ce qui est grand aux yeux de l'humanité, tout ce qui est utile aux yeux de la patrie. Partout le gouvernement fut votre guide et votre appui. Sa conduite sera constamment la même, et votre bonheur est la seule récompense à laquelle il aspire.

" Bonaparte, 1er consul de la République ordonne que la proclamation à dessus sera inserée au *Bulletin des Lois*, publiée, imprimée et affichée sans tous les departements de la République.

" Donné à Paris, au Palais du gouvernement, le 18 brumaire an X de la République Française.

      " Le 1er consul—signé, Bonaparte.

" Par le 1er consul : le secrétaire d'Etat, H. B. Maret."

D

THE Definitive Treaty of Peace between His Britannic Majesty & the French Republic, His Catholic Majesty, the Batavian Republic, Signed at Amiens, the 27th March, 1802. Published by Authority.

His Majesty the King of the United Kingdom of Great Britain and Ireland, and the First Consul of the French Republic, in the Name of the French People, being animated with an equal desire to put an end to the Calamities of War, have laid the Foundation of Peace in the Preliminary Articles signed in London, the First of October One thousand eight hundred one (Ninth *Vendémiaire*, Year Ten).

And as by the Fifteenth Article of the said Preliminaries, it has been stipulated that Plenipotentiaries should be named on each Side, who shall proceed to Amiens for the purpose of concluding a Definitive Treaty, in concert with the Allies of the contracting Powers ;

His Majesty the King of the United Kingdom of Great Britain and Ireland has named for his Plenipotentiary the Marquis Cornwallis, Knight of the most Illustrious Order of the Garter, Privy Counsellor to His Majesty, General of His Armies, &tc ; the First Consul of the French Republic, in the Name of the French People, the Citizen Joseph Bonaparte, Counsellor of State ; His Majesty the King of Spain & of the Indies, and the Government of the Batavian Republic, have named for their Plenipotentiaries, *videlicet*, His Catholic Majesty Don Joseph Nicolas de Azara, His Counsellor of State, Knight, Great Cross of the Order of Charles III. His said Majesty's Ambassador Extraordinary to the French Republic, etc, and the Government of the Batavian Republic Roger John Schimmelpenninck, their Ambassador Extraordinary to the French Republic ; who, after having duly communicated to each other their full Powers, which are transcribed at the end of the present Treaty, have agreed upon the following Articles :—

ARTICLE I

There shall be Peace, Friendship & good Understanding between His Majesty the King of the United Kingdom of Great Britain & Ireland, His Heirs & Successors, on the One Part ; and the French Republic, His Majesty the King of Spain, His Heirs & Successors, and the Batavian Republic, on the other Part. The contracting Parties shall give the greatest Attention to maintain between themselves and their States, a perfect Harmony, and without allowing, on either Side, any Kind of Hostilities, by Sea or by Land, to be committed for any Cause, or under any Pretence whatsoever.

They shall carefully avoid every Thing which might hereafter affect the Union happily reestablished, and they shall not afford any Assistance or Protection, directly or indirectly, to those who should cause Prejudice to any of them.

ARTICLE II

All the Prisoners taken on either Side, as well by Land as by Sea, and the Hostages carried away or given during the War, and to this day, shall be restored without Ransom, in Six Weeks at latest, to be computed from the Day of the Exchange of the Ratifications of the present Treaty, and on paying the Debts which shall have been contracted during their Captivity. Each contracting Party shall respectively discharge the Advances which have been made by any of the contracting Parties for the Subsistance & Maintenance of the Prisoners in the Country where they have been detained. For this purpose a Commission shall be appointed by Agreement, which shall be specially charged to ascertain & regulate the Compensation which may be due to either of the contracting Powers. The Time & Place where the Commissioners, who shall be charged with the Execution of this Article, shall assemble, shall also be fixed upon by Agreement ; and the said Commissioners shall take into account the Expences occasioned not only to the Prisoners of the respective Nations, but also by the Foreign Troops who, before they were made Prisoners, were in the Pay or at the Disposal of any of the contracting Parties.

ARTICLE III

His Britannic Majesty restores to the French Republic, and her Allies ; namely, His Catholic Majesty & the Batavian Republic, all the Possessions & Colonies which belonged to them respectively, and which had been occupied or conquered by the British Forces in the Course of the War, with the exception of the Island of Trinidad, and the Dutch Possessions in the Island of Ceylon.

ARTICLE IV

His Catholic Majesty cedes and guarantees in full Right & Sovereignty to His Britannic Majesty the Island of Trinidad.

ARTICLE V

The Batavian Republic cedes & guarantees in full Right & Sovereignty to his Britannic Majesty all the Possessions & Establishments in the Island of Ceylon, which belonged, before the War, to the Republic of the United Provinces, or to their East India Company.

Article VI

The Cape of Good Hope remains in full Sovereignty of the Batavian Republic, as it was before the War.

The Ships of every description belonging to the other contracting Parties shall have the Right to put in there, and to purchase such Supplies as they may stand in Need of as heretofore, without paying any other Duties than those to which the Ships of the Batavian Republic are subjected.

Article VII

The Territories & Possessions of Her Most Faithful Majesty are maintained in their Integrity as they were previous to the Commencement of the War.

Nevertheless the Limits of French & Portugese Guiana shall be determined by the River Arawari, which falls into the Ocean below the North Cape, near the Isle Neuve, and the Island of Penitence, above a Degree & One Third in North Latitude. Those Limits shall follow the course of the River Arawari from that of its Mouths, which is at the greatest distance from the North Cape to its Source, and thence in a direct Line from its Source to the River Branco, towards the West. The Northern Bank of the River Arawari, from its Mouth to its South, and the Lands which are situated to the North of the Line of the Limits above fixed, shall consequently belong in full Sovereignty to the French Republic. The Southern Bank of the said River from its source, and all the Lands to the Southward of the said Line of Demarcation, shall belong to his most Faithful Majesty. The Navigation of the River Arawari shall be common to both Nations.

The Arrangements which have taken Place between the Courts of Madrid and of Lisbon, for the Settlement of their Frontiers in Europe, shall, however, be executed conformably to the Treaty of Badajoz.

ARTICLE VIII

The Territories, Possessions & Rights of the Ottoman Porte, are hereby maintained in their Integrity, such as they were previous to the War.

ARTICLE IX

The Republic of the Seven Islands is hereby acknowledged.

ARTICLE X

The Islands of Malta, Gozo & Comino, shall be restored to the Order of Saint John of Jerusalem, and shall be held by it upon the same Conditions on which the Order held them previous to the War, & under the following Stipulations :—

1. The Knights of the Order, whose Langues shall continue to subsist after the Exchange of the Ratification of the present Treaty, are invited to return to Malta as soon as that Exchange shall have taken place. They shall there form a general chapter, and shall proceed to the Election of a Grand Master, to be chosen from amongst the Natives of those Nations which preserve Langues, if no such Election shall have been already made since the Exchange of the Ratification of the Preliminary Articles of Peace. It is understood that an Election which shall have been made subsequent to that Period, shall alone be considered as valid, to the Exclusion of every other which shall have taken Place at any Time previous to the said Period.

2. The Governments of Great Britain & of the French Republic, being desirous of placing the Order of Saint John, and the Island of Malta, in a State of entire Independence on each of those Powers, do

agree that there shall be no English nor French
Langues ; and that no Individual belonging to either
of the said Powers, shall be admissable into the
Order.

3. A Maltese shall be established to be supported
out of the Land Revenue & commercial Duties of
the Island. There shall be Dignities, with Appoint-
ments, and an Auberge appropriated to this Langue ;
no Proofs of Nobility shall be necessary for the
Admission of Knights into the said Langue ; they
shall be competent to hold every Office, and to
enjoy every Privilege in the like Manner as the
Knights of the other Langues. The Municipal,
Revenue, Civil, Judicial, and other Offices under
the Government of the Island shall be filled, at least
in the Proportion of One Half, by native inhabitants
of Malta, Gozo & Comino.

4. The forces of his Britannic Majesty shall
evacuate the Island and its Dependencies within
Three Months after the Exchange of the Ratifications, or sooner if it can be done : at that Period the
Island shall be delivered up to the Order in the State
in which it now is—provided that the Grand Master,
or Commissioners, fully empowered according to the
Statutes of the Order, be upon the Island to receive
Possession ; and that the Force to be furnished by
His Sicilian Majesty, as hereinafter stipulated, be
arrived there.

5. The Garrison of the Island shall, at all Times,
consist at least One Half of Native Maltese ; and
the Order shall have the Liberty of recruiting for
the Remainder of the Garrison from the Natives of
those Countries only that shall continue to possess
Langues. The Native Maltese Troops shall be

officered by Maltese, and the supreme Command of the Garrison, as well as the Appointment of the Officers, shall be vested in the Grand Master of the Order ; and he shall not be at Liberty to divest himself of it, even for a Time, except in Favour of a Knight of the Order, and in consequence of the Opinion of the Council of the Order.

6. The Independence of the Islands of Malta, Gozo & Comino, as well as the present Arrangement, shall be under the Protection & Guarantee of Great Britain, France, Austria, Russia, Spain & Prussia.

7. The perpetual Neutrality of the Order & of the Island of Malta, and its Dependencies, is hereby declared.

8. The Ports of Malta shall be open to the Commerce & Navigation of all Nations, who shall pay equal & moderate Duties. These Duties shall be applied to the Support of the Maltese Langue, in the manner specified in Paragraph 3, to that of the Civil & Military Establishments of the Island, & to that of a Lazaretto, open to all Flags.

9. The Barbary States are excepted from the Provisions of the Two preceding Paragraphs, until by means of an Arrangement to be made by the contracting Parties, the System of Hostility, which subsists between the said Barbary States, the Order of St John, and the Powers possessing Langues, or taking Part in the Formation of them, shall be terminated.

10. The Order shall be governed both in Spiritual & Temporal Matters, by the same Statutes that were in force at the Time when the Knights quitted the

Island, so far as the same shall not be derogated from by the present Treaty.

11. The Stipulations contained in Paragraphs 3, 5, 7, 8, and 10, shall be converted into Laws and perpetual Statutes of the Order, in the customary Manner. And the Grand Master (or if he should not be in the Island at the Time of its Restitution to the Order, his Representative), as well as his Successors, shall be bound to make Oath to observe them punctually.

12. His Sicilian Majesty shall be invited to furnish Two thousand Men, Natives of his Dominions, to serve as a Garrison for the several Fortresses upon the Island. This Force shall remain there for One Year from the Period of the Restitution of the Island to the Knights ; after the Expiration of which Term, if the Order of St John shall not, in the Opinion of the guarantying Powers, have raised a sufficient Force to garrison the Island & its Dependencies, in the Manner provided in Paragraph 5, the Neapolitan Troops shall remain, until they shall be relieved by another Force, judged to be sufficient by the said Powers.

13. The severeral Powers specified in Paragraph 6, *videliciet*, Great Britain, France, Austria, Russia, Spain & Prussia, shall be invited to accede to the present Arrangement.

ARTICLE XI

The French Forces shall evacuate the Kingdom of Naples & the Roman Territory ; the English Forces shall in like manner evacuate Porto Ferrajo, and generally all the Ports & Islands which they occupy in the Mediterranean or in the Adriatic.

Article XII

The Evacuations, Cessions & Restitutions, stipulated for by the present Treaty, except where otherwise expressly provided for, shall take place in Europe within One Month ; in the Continent & Seas of America, and of Africa, within Three Months ; and in the Continent & Seas of Asia, within Six Months, after the Ratification of the present Definitive Treaty.

Article XIII

In all the Cases of Restitution agreed upon by the present Treaty, the Fortifications shall be delivered up in the State in which they may have been at the Time of the Signature of the Preliminary Treaty ; and all the Works which shall have been constructed since the Occupation, shall remain untouched.

It is farther agreed, that in all the Cases of Cession stipulated, there shall be allowed to the Inhabitants, of whatever Condition or Nation they may be, a Term of Three Years, to be computed from the Notification of this present Treaty, for the Purpose of disposing of their Property acquired or possessed either before or during the War, in which Term of Three Years they may have the free Exercise of their Religion & Enjoyment of their Property.

The same Privilege is granted in the Countries restored to all those, whether Inhabitants or others, who shall have made therein any Establishments whatsoever during the Time when those Countries were in the possession of Great Britain.

With respect to the Inhabitants of the Countries restored or ceded, it is agreed that none of them shall be prosecuted, disturbed, or molested in their Persons or Properties under any Pretext, on Account of their Conduct or political Opinions, or of their Attachment to any of the contracting Powers, nor on any other Account, except that of Debts contracted to Individuals, or on Account of Acts posterior to the Present Treaty.

ARTICLE XIV

All Sequestrations imposed by any of the Parties on the funded Property, Revenues, or Debts of whatsoever Description, belonging to any of the contracting Powers, or to their Subjects or Citizens, shall be taken off immediately after the Signature of the Definite Treaty. The Decision of all Claims brought forward by Individuals, the Subjects or Citizens of any of the contracting Powers respectively, against Individuals, Subjects or Citizens of any of the others, for Rights, Debts, Property, or Effects whatsoever, which, according to received Usages & the Law of Nations ought to revive at the Period of Peace, shall be heard and decided before competent Tribunals; and in all Cases prompt & ample Justice shall be administered in the Countries where the Claims are made.

ARTICLE XV

The Fisheries on the Coast of Newfoundland, and of the adjacent Islands, and of the Gulf of St Lawrence, are replaced on the same footing on which they were previous to the War; the French Fishermen & the Inhabitants of Saint Pierre & Miquelon shall have the Privilege of cutting such Wood as they may stand in Need of in the Bays of Fortune & Despair, for the Space of One Year from the date of the Notification of the present Treaty.

ARTICLE XVI

In order to prevent all Causes of Complaint & Dispute which may arise on account of Prizes which may have been made at Sea, after the Signature of the Preliminary Articles, it is reciprocally agreed that the Vessels & Effects which may have been taken in the British Channel, and in the North Sea after the space of Twelve Days, to be computed from the Exchange of the Ratifications of the said Preliminary Articles, shall be restored on either Side ; that the term shall be One Month from the British Channel & the North Seas, as far as the Canary Islands inclusively, whether in the Ocean or in the Mediterranean ; Two Months from the said Canary Islands as far as the Equator ; and lastly Five Months in all other Parts of the World, without any Exception, or any more particular Description of Time or Place

Article XVII

The Ambassadors, Ministers, and other agents of the contracting Powers, shall enjoy respectively in the States of the said Powers, the same Rank, Privileges, Prerogatives, and Immunities, which Public Agents of the same Class enjoyed previous to the War.

Article XVIII

The Branch of the House of Nassau, which was established in the Republic formerly called the Republic of the United Provinces, and now the Batavian Republic, having suffered losses there, as well in private Property as in consequence of the Change of Constitution adopted in that Country, an adequate Compensation shall be procured for the said Branch of the House of Nassan for the said Losses.

Article XIX

The present Definitive Treaty of Peace is declared common to the Sublime Ottoman Porte, the Ally of His Britannic Majesty ; and the Sublime Porte shall be invited to transmit its Act of Accession thereto, in the shortest Delay possible.

ARTICLE XX

It is agreed that the Contracting Parties shall, on Requisition made by them respectively, or by their Ministers or Officers duly authorized to make the same, deliver up to Justice, Persons accused of the Crimes of Murder, Forgery, or fraudulent Bankruptcy, committed within the Jurisdiction of the requiring Party ; provided that this shall be done only when the Evidence of the Criminality shall be so authenticated as that the Laws of the Country where the person so accused shall be found, would justify his Apprehension & Commitment for Trial, if the Offence had been there committed. The Expenses of such Apprehension & Delivery shall be borne & defrayed by those who make the Requisition. It is understood that this Article does not regard in any Manner Crimes of Murder, Forgery, or fraudulent Bankruptcy committed antecedently to the Conclusion of the Definitive Treaty.

ARTICLE XXI

The Contracting Parties promise to observe sincerely & *bonâ fide* all the Articles contained in the present Treaty ; and they will not suffer the same to be infringed, directly or indirectly, by their respective Subjects or Citizens ; and the said contracting Parties generally & reciprocally guaranty to each other all the Stipulations of the present Treaty.

ARTICLE XXII

The present Treaty shall be ratified by the Contracting Parties in Thirty Days, or sooner if possible, and the Ratification shall be exchanged in due Form at Paris.

In Witness whereof, we, the underwritten Plenipotentiaries, have signed with our Hands, and in virtue of our respective Full Powers, the present